GHOSTS OF THE AMERICAN REVOLUTION

GHOSTS OF THE AMERICAN REVOLUTION

Sam Baltrusis

Guilford, Connecticut

Globe
Pequot

An imprint of Globe Pequot, the trade division of The Rowman & Littlefield Publishing Group, Inc.
4501 Forbes Blvd., Ste. 200
Lanham, MD 20706
www.rowman.com

Distributed by NATIONAL BOOK NETWORK

British Library Cataloguing in Publication Information available

Library of Congress Cataloging-in-Publication Data available

ISBN 978-1-4930-5174-8 (paper)
ISBN 978-1-4930-5175-5 (electronic)

CONTENTS

FOREWORD

We're still discovering the bones of our past buried in basements and backyards. These accounts give them life.
—Roxie Zwicker, AUTHOR AND TOUR GUIDE

What comes to mind when you hear the phrase "full of spirit?" Do you think of someone who is full of energy, or perhaps the phrase brings to mind someone who is courageous? To delve into the realms of the unknown, eagerly pull the veil to the side and explore the topic of ghosts and the American Revolution as it awakens visions of the birth of a nation.

Those courageous people who cried out for liberty were stepping into the unknown in a different way, but with a strong conviction in what they believed. The "shot heard round the world" during the Battle of Concord and Lexington in 1775 still echoes throughout the region today and along with it are the spirits of those who were there and fighting for independence.

In between the gleaming towers of steel and along the blacktop ribbons of roadways crisscrossing New England there are signs and simple reminders of what happened at that spot and who lived or traveled through there. Passing by these markers we become disconnected from our past and the spirit of place is not fully realized or appreciated.

Some of these historic plaques tell us we are standing at a point of assembly, where citizen soldiers gathered and then marched, with heavy gear, hundreds of miles to answer the call of the American Revolution. Other plaques tell stories of unthinkable missions such as the long transport of sixty tons of cannons and weapons captured at Fort Ticonderoga and transported 300 miles to Boston during the winter through rough woods and waters.

If we aren't seeing the reminders of our history in plain sight, we could be missing the spirits that linger there as well.

There are so many opportunities to be guided to our Revolutionary War past. There are trails, historic sites, homes, memorials, burial grounds with humble graveside flags. Does the voice of the past call to us in these places? Should we search for the reasons why these spirits remain?

By looking further into these ghostly occurrences, additional chapters of our history are revealed to us. The lives of those who witnessed and struggled through a time that affected every citizen and household. Thousands of troops, clashing on foot and battling with militiamen, along with men, women, and children standing firm in what seemed like impossible odds. Death came so swiftly to some that they were buried where they died without any ceremony.

Some names in this book might be ones you recognize or perhaps even stand out. These accounts you are about to read prompt you to connect in a way you may have not considered before. A glimpse of a passing redcoat soldier in downtown Boston might be startling at first but then many questions come to mind. *What do the spirits want and why are they still here?*

Whether we're connected by blood or spirit, each of us today are living the freedoms in which these people were fighting to uphold. We are already connected to the past, even if we aren't completely conscious of it. I've personally noticed that when I'm talking about New England's history during the Revolution with someone who is not from the region, they offer a fresh perspective and different appreciation than those who have lived here their entire lives.

The questions visitors ask and the attention they give to the people and stories remind me of how lucky I am to be born and raised in this historic region. I live within a mile of several buildings that George Washington toured. I drive past a church bell every day that was forged by Paul Revere, and there's a lightning rod by Benjamin Franklin on a nearby house. I want to know more about these people, their life, death, and afterlife in some cases. You will often hear me say at a historic site, "I wish I was there to see what they saw."

In author Sam Baltrusis's *Ghosts of the American Revolution*, he not only presents an opportunity to explore these moments in time, but also gives a voice to those who were there. We're still discovering the bones of our past buried in basements and backyards. These accounts give them life. Our beliefs give them purpose, and that's one of the many ways to not only connect with our history but to honor it.

—Roxie Zwicker, *New England Curiosities*

Signing of the Declaration of Independence in Philadelphia, Pennsylvania, on July 4, 1776. *Courtesy Deposit Photos*

INTRODUCTION

Was the mob mentality responsible for the execution of twenty inno-cent people during the Salem witch trials also the underlying fuel used during the Revolutionary War less than a century later?

It's the 250-year anniversary of the Boston Massacre and I'm standing in the middle of a mob of angry protestors gathered outside of the Old State House. The chilly March event was supposed to be a recreation of the pivotal standoff in 1770, but it oddly doesn't feel that way.

Despite being surrounded by obvious reminders that it's 2020, the vibe seems like I'm actually watching an important historic event unfold. Somehow, I've been transported back in time.

People in the crowds were shouting "go back to England," "scoun-drels," and one overzealous local next to me called the incoming British sentry "lobsters" and "bloody backs." Before the commemoration started, I was told by an actor portraying a wealthy Boston merchant that things were about to get real. "We are trying to be as accurate as possible with-out actually killing each other," he said with a laugh. Boy, was he right.

As a group of redcoat reenactors fired off their fake Flintlock mus-kets and church bells chimed over the loudspeaker, I tried my best to connect with the spirits of the five murdered colonists using my trusty dowsing rods. No luck. I didn't get a response.

At that moment, however, I did have an epiphany while standing in a sea of frenzied "no taxation without representation" spectators in down-town Boston. Even though it was a reenactment, the mock militiamen were out for blood.

The scene struck a nerve. Reliving the Boston Massacre exactly two-and-a-half centuries later was an eye-opening display of the aggressive male psyche gone awry. I've been down this path before. We were cele-brating mob violence.

For years, my focus as a paranormal researcher and historian has been on Salem, Massachusetts, and the horrors that unfolded during the witch trials of 1692. As someone who has been based in the Boston area for

Built in 1713, the Old State House was the backdrop for the Boston Massacre on March 5, 1770. *Courtesy Deposit Photos*

most of my adult life, I've ignored the ghosts of the American Revolution literally lurking in my own backyard.

Patriotic phantoms and residual redcoats? Yes, we have them.

The word *huzzah,* an old-school exclamation expressing approval or delight during the colonial era, wasn't even on my word-choice radar until it inexplicably came up during an impromptu spirit box session near my home outside of Boston.

It happened on Prospect Hill in Somerville's Union Square. I was checking out reports that the recent construction outside of the historic landmark was stirring up spirits. Somehow, I picked up the word *huzzah* on my fancy, ghost-hunting device. Why?

The creepy castle atop Somerville's historic Prospect Hill oozes a "something wicked this way comes" vibe. Built in 1902 to commemorate the hill's role as a Revolutionary War fortification, the castle boasts killer views of the Boston skyline. It was its bird's-eye location that supposedly attracted George Washington, then the Continental army's commander in-chief, to the site as he hashed out plans for the Siege of Boston. "From the summit of the hill, an extensive view of the surrounding country could be obtained, thus affording an excellent opportunity to note movements of the opposing forces. Immediate preparations were made to erect fortifications, beginning at a point near Union Square and extending over the hill," wrote Albert Haskell in his *Historical Guidebook of Somerville.* "After the Battle of Bunker Hill the Americans withdrew to this hill, taking shelter behind the earthworks."

Historians claim that Washington raised an early version of the American flag, called the Grand Union Flag, on January 1, 1776. However, it's up for debate whether this momentous event—which was reportedly greeted with cheers and a thirteen-gun salute—was in fact the country's first flag raising. We do know the initial flag was transferred to a fort in Boston Harbor after the British retreated.

For the record, the Patriots in Prospect Hill yelled "huzzah" when the flag was raised. Yes, the mystery surrounding my EVP session near my home was solved.

In addition to its glory days as a pre–Revolutionary War fortification, the so-called citadel has a dark history as a makeshift prison for British general John Burgoyne's Hessian troops, hired German mercenaries shipped over to Boston and used as guns for hire.

Apparently, it was a tough winter for the prisoners of war, who had a helluva time finding wood for heat. "The British and Hessian soldiers, while in Somerville, were quartered in the old barracks left by the Americans after the Siege of Boston," wrote Charles Darwin Elliot in *Somerville's History*. "The wind whistled through the thin walls, the rain came through the roofs, the snow lay in drifts on the floor," complained one prisoner of war cited in Elliot's book.

General Friedrich Adolf Riedesel, Burgoyne's wingman and general of the German troops, echoed the complaints. "Indeed the greater number of the soldiers are so miserably lodged that they are unable to shelter themselves from the cold and rain in this severe season of the year," Riedesel noted in his diary. "The soldiers, of whom twenty to twenty-four occupy the same barrack, are without light at night. Three of them share a bed," he continued, adding that they were imprisoned in squalor for an entire year, beginning in winter 1777 to November 1778.

Of course, the haunted "huzzah!" experience in Somerville wasn't my first face-to-face encounter with the ghosts of the American Revolution.

One night, when I was setting up for a book signing at the church next to Cambridge's Old Burying Point, I had a close encounter with an unseen force. The back door, which was oddly propped open by one of the cemetery's gravestones, mysteriously closed. I heard what sounded like the floorboards creaking and then a second door slammed shut. I looked up and spotted something, or someone, out of the corner of my eye. He looked like a redcoat and he was wearing a tricorn hat. I held my breath.

At this point, I didn't know about the legend surrounding Lieutenant Richard Brown, a British soldier who was shot in the face in 1777 by a Patriot sentry while descending Prospect Hill in Somerville. He was buried in the Vassall tomb and allegedly haunts Christ Church, which also abuts the Old Burying Ground. Apparently, his interment was so controversial that hundreds of crazed colonists ransacked the historic Anglican church. Brown's spirit reportedly slams doors and blows out candles.

Was my encounter at the church a ghost? Possibly. However, I do believe in residual hauntings or a videotape-like replay of a traumatic event that occurred years ago. My theory is that Cambridge's Old Burying Ground is full of skeletal secrets, an energy vortex of unjust killings and unmarked graves dating back to the days leading up to the Revolutionary War.

For several years, I produced a ghost tour in Harvard Square and we had repeated sightings and hard-to-explain photos shot in the area believed to be Cambridge's haunted corridor. Most of the guides on the ghost walk agreed that the starting point, the Old Burying Point, was one of the most paranormally active spots on the tour.

Based on my first-hand experience with the British soldier ghost, I have to agree. The city is wicked haunted.

Known for its prestigious universities, Cambridge became an unlikely pre–Revolutionary War hotspot. There was, however, little indication of this overnight upheaval in the early 1700s. Its Sleepy Hollow–esque vibe, modeled after the picturesque English villages its Puritan founders had left behind, turned into chaos as nine thousand citizen soldiers from rustic country towns scattered throughout New England gathered in the Cambridge Common in 1775. Before the "shot heard round the world" in Concord on April 29, Cambridge boasted about two thousand residents, ninety percent of whom were descendants of the seven hundred Puritans who had sailed from England to Newtowne in 1630.

According to legend, General George Washington assumed his role as commander of the thousands of militiamen known as the Continental army beneath an elm tree in the Common. This epic scene, which has been immortalized by illustrators and storytellers over the years, is believed to be more myth than fact. According to Richard Ketchum's *The World of George Washington*, the emerging leader was concerned with his crew of untrained militiamen, calling them a "mixed multitude of people . . . under very little discipline, order or government."

In other words, Washington had his work cut out for him.

The sudden upheaval in 1775 is believed to be the source of some of the residual energy that left a psychic imprint on the weathered streets and centuries-old buildings in Harvard Square. According to master psychic Denise Fix, a handful of Cambridge's ghosts can be traced back to the American War of Independence. "Some of the spirits around us are

Author Sam Baltrusis investigated many of the haunted locations featured in *Ghosts of the American Revolution. Photo by Frank C. Grace*

wearing uniforms," Fix told me during a visit to Cambridge's Old Burying Ground. "There's a lot of residual energy associated with men from George Washington's era. I keep seeing men wearing [tricorn] hats."

Are the tricorn hat-wearing ghosts from Cambridge's Revolutionary War past still lingering? Yes. Paranormal investigators like Adam Berry from *Kindred Spirits* believe residual energy associated with this tumultuous time in American history may have left a supernatural imprint. "Anytime there's a traumatic event, it could be left behind," Berry said. "If you walk into a room and two people have been arguing, fiercely, you can feel that weirdness they've created or energy they emit spewing at each other. I do think there's a form of energy that can be left behind from a traumatic event or any kind of murder or suicide in a room. The theory is that maybe that energy goes into the walls and lingers there."

When it comes to the American Revolution's lingering psychic imprint, all paths lead to the corner of Massachusetts Avenue and Garden Street. Known as "God's Acre," the Old Burying Ground was established before 1635 and preceded both Christ Church and First Parish. Harvard presidents and paupers were buried there.

Cambridge was known as Newtowne until 1638, and the town's oldest cemetery was rumored to be around Brattle and Ash Streets. It's long gone. "It was deemed that the cemetery was not safe from the intrusion of wild animals, and the cemetery was not used after 1634," wrote Roxie Zwicker in *Massachusetts Book of the Dead*. "There is no indication of where the cemetery is in the city today, as it has been lost to time and urban development."

As the only burial spot for nearly two hundred years, the Old Burying Ground received a cross section of the population, including two enslaved men, Neptune Frost and Cato Stedman, who fought and died in the Battle of Bunker Hill and at least nineteen additional Revolutionary War soldiers. Burial spaces in the early years weren't permanently marked, and the cemetery contains more remains than what has been reported.

Most of the monuments are slate headstones, and some markers, including those crafted by Joseph Lamson from Charlestown, portray "evil demons of death" with imps carrying coffins away. The oldest gravestone, dated 1653, belongs to Anne Erinton, but the stone may have been placed later, as headstones didn't come into general use until the 1670s. Excluding the tombs, the cemetery's last known burial was in 1811.

There's also a subterranean tunnel. As in Britain, upper-class families wished to be interred in burial vaults rather than in caskets placed directly in the ground. The John Vassall tomb is the most elaborate. Last opened in 1862, it contained twenty-five caskets, including that of Andrew Craigie, who acquired the family's Christ Church pew and burial plot along with the Vassall estate in 1792.

Mythology surrounding the Vassall family continues to intrigue historians. Penelope Vassall, who fled Cambridge during the Revolutionary War, supposedly paid twenty pounds in 1722 to free the child of her driver Tony from slavery. "Cambridge, becoming a military camp, was neither a pleasant nor safe residence for those who still adhered to King George, so Madame Vassall departed in haste to Antigua," wrote Dorothy Dudley in *Theatrum Majorum*. "Popular tradition asserts that the slaves of the Vassalls were inhumanely treated. There seems to be no foundation for this report."

Vassall visited Cambridge after the war and the Loyalist was buried in the subterranean vault beneath Christ Church. She was joined by Tony's son Darby Vassall, an African-American man, who was eventually freed from slavery. He was the last person to be interred in the tomb on October 15, 1861.

Leave it to Cambridge to challenge the status quo. But was the haunted city socially conscious during the colonial era? According to Gavin W. Kleespies, the former executive director of the Cambridge Historical Society, not really.

"I would be hesitant to say that Cambridge was more progressive back then," explained Kleespies, now the director of programs at the Massachusetts Historical Society. "You have people like Cotton Mather coming out of Cambridge and then heading off to Salem during the witch hysteria. His father, Increase Mather, was a Puritan leader and administrator at Harvard. They both accused innocent people of witchcraft and then sent them to prison, and some of them were held in Cambridge."

Apparently, "the prison was atrocious" and housed many women, including Goody Elizabeth Kendall, who were wrongly accused of witchcraft. Kendall was believed to be executed at Gallows Hill, in North Cambridge, during the 1692 witch trials hysteria. Kleespies, a Cambridge native who returned to his hometown in 2008, said the city didn't become a center for progressive thought until the late eighteenth century. "Puritan New England was horrifying in many ways," he continued. "I wouldn't say there was a blood lust, but there was definitely a callousness back then."

Newtowne was founded on September 30, 1630, when the deputy governor of the Massachusetts Bay Company, Thomas Dudley, was on the hunt for a "fit place for a fortified town." He convinced John Winthrop, the first governor of the colony, that the land surrounding present-day Harvard Square was an ideal spot. "Newtowne didn't last that long as the state capital," Kleespies said. "Cambridge didn't quite know what to do for a long time until 1636, when Harvard was founded. It gave Cambridge an economic purpose, and it quickly became the place to go to college in colonial America."

Kleespies said early Cambridge was a typical Puritan New England village town for almost a century. "By the mid-1730s, Cambridge started developing as a resort with country estates for wealthy merchants from Boston. The way to get from Boston to Cambridge was over the Great Bridge, and it wasn't something they could do on foot in a short period of time. So these country estates for wealthy merchants were built, and it slowly became Tory Row."

Cambridge became a hub of activity as anti-British sentiment started to escalate. George Washington, who stayed in Cambridge for almost one year, assumed his role as the leader of the troops on July 3, 1775. British general John Burgoyne, who retreated with troops after losing the Battle of Saratoga in 1777, was held prisoner in Cambridge. Apparently, the British soldiers weren't treated well.

"One of the officers from the Convention Troops was shot in the face and killed because he didn't stop when a sentry told him to," said Kleespies, alluding to Lieutenant Richard Brown, whose spirit allegedly

The equestrian statue of George Washington is located in Boston's Public Garden. *Courtesy Deposit Photos*

haunts Christ Church. "When he had his funeral at the church, the townspeople ransacked it. I mean, it was a funeral. They were supposed to be given proper quarters, and the officers were European gentlemen and they weren't expecting to be sleeping in a pub."

Burgoyne spent several not-so-stellar nights at the Blue Anchor Tavern in Winthrop Square before convincing Cambridge's leaders to move him into the more posh Apthorp House. "As far as the treatment of their prisoners of war, Cambridge has a really bad reputation," continued Kleespies. "It was shocking. These soldiers were expecting to be treated with a certain degree of civility, and they were thrown out in the street. And then a Patriot shot one of their members in the face. Unbelievable."

Apparently, the cruel-and-unusual punishments directed toward the Loyalists during the fight for independence was also the norm in Boston, Massachusetts, as well. Yes, the Patriots were out for blood.

Brooke Barbier, author of *Boston in the American Revolution: A Town Versus an Empire*, told me that it's important to understand that there are two sides to every story. "There were Loyalists in Boston and they were typically the richest. We need to hear their voices too. In some cases, the Loyalists were severely mistreated," the author and the Ye Olde Tavern Tour owner said. "One of the Loyalists suffered what was called Hillsborough paint, which means his home was covered in feces and urine. In some cases, the Loyalists were mistreated to an extreme so it's important to tell that side of the story too. It was not a steady march to the revolution. It was messy and it was complicated."

Like tar and feathering? "Yes, that happened," she said. "Something I want to clear up, it wasn't scalding, hot tar. It was a warm tar that actually lifted the top layer of skin and then feathers were put on them. Then, they were paraded around Boston, or whatever colonial town they were in. Tar and feathering weren't meant to hurt you physically. It was meant to embarrass you. Shame was a powerful motivator."

Barbier said the key players of the American Revolution—the villains and the victims—are often remembered using black-and-white thinking. Yes, to err is human. "People reacted in a way that people today would react if they were in a similar situation. They could be jealous, fearful, or angry."

When Barbier talked about the Puritan approach to public shaming, it reminded me of the Salem witch trials. Many of the innocents executed were paraded in oxcarts en route to the gallows on Proctor's Ledge. It was as if the people of Salem were presenting these innocent men and women as cautionary tales.

As Barbier was discussing the slow build leading up to the American Revolution, I had the ultimate realization: The scrappy spirit of the colonial revolt wasn't a far cry from the horrors that unfolded in 1692.

"Mobs, and mob violence, was a socially acceptable way during that time to address your grievances," Barbier explained. "It actually came from England. The colonists were being good British subjects and following in their forefathers' footsteps by violently rebelling. It wasn't until it became more spirited and consistent that it was a problem for parliament. People were improvising and using tools they've used for decades, and then it became something bigger as this tension started to build."

Was the mob mentality responsible for the execution of twenty innocent people during the witch-trials hysteria in Salem also the underlying fuel used during the Revolutionary War less than a century later?

Yes. The same Puritan-bred patriarchy that gave rise to our country ... also hunted witches. Like the Salem witch trials, the American Revolution is stained with blood and its ghosts are still lurking in the shadows seeking postmortem revenge.

MANHATTAN'S SPIRITS OF '76

*We had to actually stop the investigation to inspect the house and
make sure that no one broke into the mansion.*
        —Angela Artuso, Gotham Paranormal Research Society

It's Halloween night in New York City and the veil between the
living and the dead had officially lifted. The spirits of Manhattan
were walking among the costumed revelers exploring various neigh-
borhoods as my bus from Boston pulled into Port Authority. The
city was electric.

The newly built Staypineapple Hotel in Midtown was a short
walk from the station. I managed to navigate my way through the
crowds of trick-or-treaters parading up and down Eighth Avenue.
I was looking forward to spending the night relaxing in my not-
haunted hotel on West 36th Street.

I needed a ghost break. No luck.

Freddy, the hotel's night-shift employee, welcomed me into
the lobby. As he was checking me in, a man wearing an old-school
ghost costume, a white sheet with glasses, walked by. The Halloween prankster poked his head into the lobby and he waved at
both of us and then jokingly said, "Boo" with a thick Long Island
accent. Freddy and I both laughed.

"This hotel isn't haunted, right?" I sheepishly asked. Freddy
paused. "Well, it can get creepy late at night, especially when the
outside noise from the traffic and pedestrians on the street quiet
down," he said. "I sometimes hear what sounds like a person
walking down the stairs. I will be standing in the lobby, expecting
someone to walk by. But there's no one there."

Phantom footsteps? Yep, the supposedly not-haunted hotel
probably has ghostly guests. It figures.

Freddy showed me the stairwell where he often hears the
mysterious noises from beyond. It's a fire exit and I cautiously
inspected the area.

After touring the potentially haunted hallway with Freddy,
I walked around the property, dodging the late-night Halloween
partygoers as they headed toward the subway. Why would this new
Midtown Manhattan hotel have paranormal activity? I looked up
and noticed the English Gothic-style building across the street.

Bull's-eye! I was looking at the façade of the historic Christ Church. In fact, the century-old structure had a past life as the only Presbyterian place of worship in this predominantly Catholic neighborhood between Eighth and Ninth Avenues.

"The church fed the poor, tended to the working-class neighborhood's often tuberculosis-stricken sick, and offered refuge and entertainment to soldiers during both world wars," reported Steve Cuozzo in the October 27, 2016, edition of the *New York Post.* "It hosted loud labor rallies as sweat-baked garment factories began pushing out the area's smaller apartment buildings."

These types of activities tend to leave a psychic imprint at the "holy haunts" I've investigated in the past. Haunted churches? Yes, it's common.

While people find solace in places of worship, the emotions associated with important events—like a marriage or a baptism—can linger within these hallowed and often historic walls. "In some Catholic churches, for example, nuns and priests devote their entire lives to serving the church and spend countless hours each week in prayer, teaching or maintaining their church as part of their devotion to God," explained tour guide Beth Rupert in her book, *Wichita Haunts.* "It is believed this energy and these repetitive actions can be captured as a residual haunt in a church."

Christ Church was slated to be completely demolished in 2014. However, a New York City developer decided to save the exterior of this extremely ornate church and transform the property into a twenty-six-floor hotel. The paranormal activity is likely a residual haunting, or a videotaped replay of a past event possibly associated with the former inhabitants of this historic church. Mystery solved.

After checking out the church-turned-hotel across the street, I continued chatting with Freddy and told him I was in New York City to work on a book about the city's lingering ghosts associated with the American Revolution. "We have plenty of them," he told me without missing a beat. "I live in Brooklyn so I know about the Revolutionary War history in my neighborhood. Did you hear about the prison ships?"

I did know a bit about the American soldiers kept in horrific conditions on a ship called the *Jersey.* The "ghost ship" was docked in Wallabout Bay in an area near modern-day Brooklyn Navy Yard. There were sixteen of these prison ships during the American Revolution.

The Statue of Liberty is a copper, neoclassical sculpture on Liberty Island in New York Harbor. *Photo by Jason Baker*

But, the *Jersey* was literally hell on earth.

While I knew the prisoners were kept in less-than-stellar conditions, I didn't know there were thousands of deaths caused by all sorts of illnesses like smallpox, dysentery, and even gangrene. Of course, many of the prisoners were murdered by the British prison guards.

According to Robert P. Watson, author of *The Ghost Ship of Brooklyn*, the death toll topped 11,500. "This ship, the *Jersey*, the 'ghost ship,' was the single bloodiest conflict of the entire Revolutionary War," Watson told the *New York Post* on August 27, 2017. "Not Saratoga, not Trenton, not Yorktown, not Germantown. The single bloodiest conflict was on board this one ship."

While the floating dungeon did hold a few American soldiers, many of the prisoners on the *Jersey* were privateers, or pirates, responsible for raiding British merchants and evading taxes. For the record, New York played a pivotal role throughout the American Revolution because of its central location within the colonies and its thriving ports. New Yorkers were extremely upset once the

Stamp Act was passed in 1765 because it imposed a tax on any paper products like newspapers or playing cards. The act threatened the economic growth of the thriving center of commerce.

Fast-forward a decade and the British converted their decommissioned warship from the Royal Navy into a floating concentration camp. "This was the statistic that knocked me out of my seat," Watson said. "Twice as many Americans died on this one ship than died in combat during the entirety of the Revolutionary War from 1775 to 1783."

Watson told the *New York Post* that the British "saw this ship as a psychological weapon of terror" and designed the floating dungeons to "deter Patriots from picking up arms against them." However, their plan backfired. Patriots heard about the atrocities happening on board the *Jersey* and it ended up fueling the fire needed to win the Revolutionary War.

Long after the British fled New York, the ghost ship eventually sank into the Wallabout Bay and the skeletal remains of the thousands who died washed ashore in Brooklyn. The bones were collected and then interred in a crypt in the 1800s. The Prison Ship Martyrs' Monument was erected to honor the fallen victims in Brooklyn's Fort Greene Park and the tower overlooks the East River.

I remembered seeing the monument when I lived in Brooklyn years ago. Even though my apartment was near the park, I had no idea the borough served as the staging area for the Battle of Long Island. More than three hundred rebel soldiers died in this bloody campaign fought on August 27, 1776.

Believe it or not, I only knew the basics about Manhattan's Revolutionary War past even though I lived in New York City for almost a decade.

I initially headed to Boston in the early 1990s to attend college. When a friend from school transferred to New York University, she invited me to visit and encouraged me to check out the Washington Square Park parade of freaks during Halloween. It was edgier back then and I remember larger-than-life puppets and furry, four-legged creatures parading through NYC's "haunted corridor."

I was smitten with the Big Apple. It was love at first bite.

After an internship at *Newsweek,* which precipitated a move to Manhattan and then my first job working at ABC Radio, I became an associate producer and worked on several national television shows for networks under the Viacom umbrella including VH1 and MTV from the mid-1990s until 2004. When I was younger, I remember walking with my friends in the heart of Times Square at night and intuitively knowing I would someday live in the city that never sleeps.

A lot has changed over the past two decades in NYC. For me, the most unexpected twist was the renewed interest in Manhattan's Revolutionary War history thanks to the success of the musical *Hamilton*.

Who knew George Washington's right-hand man could be so entertaining?

After a sleepless night watching Halloween programs in my possibly haunted hotel room in Midtown and saying goodbye to

The Morris-Jumel Mansion was built in 1765 and is considered to be one of Manhattan's most haunted locations. *Courtesy Deposit Photos*

my new friend Freddy, I woke up early on the Day of the Dead to explore a few historical haunts with ties to NYC's role in the War of Independence.

My first stop was the Morris-Jumel Mansion in Washington Heights. And, yes, the oldest house in Manhattan is also believed to be the city's most haunted.

Christopher Davalos, the mansion's director of visitor services and engagement, told me the ghosts of the American Revolution are still lingering in the shadows of the Morris-Jumel Mansion. Built in 1765 as a summer house by Colonel Roger Morris, the family abandoned the property during the outbreak of the Revolutionary War. Soon after the "shot heard round the world" on April 18, 1775, General George Washington and his rebel cohorts set up shop at Mount Morris from September to October of 1776.

"Washington was here for more than a month," Davalos said, adding that the killer views from the mansion made the location ideal for observing troop movements. "After Washington won the Battle of Harlem Heights, he was forced to retreat to the White Plains area," he said.

Mount Morris was then used by both the British and Hessian troops for the remainder of the war. It was during this time that a Hessian soldier was said to have fatally tripped on his bayonet while walking up the stairs.

When I asked Davalos if the Hessian soldier haunts the Morris-Jumel Mansion, he nodded. "Yes, he's still here," he said. "He hangs out upstairs along with the other spirits still lingering in the mansion."

While Davalos was talking, I psychically picked up what seemed like a drunken sailor. I started to sway back and forth in the first-floor foyer area of the mansion. "There are so many layers to the hauntings here," he said. "It was a tavern for a while, so it would make sense that you're picking up someone intoxicated."

After the British fled New York City on November 25, 1783, the estate was confiscated. The property then had a short stint as a local watering hole. The tavern closed almost as soon as it opened, but the structure's famous former tenant from the Revolutionary War wanted one last hurrah.

Washington, who became president in 1789, returned to the place where he scored his first victory during the American Revolution. The president met with his newly formed cabinet at the mansion on July 10, 1790.

Re-creation of George Washington's office at the Morris-Jumel Mansion in Manhattan. *Courtesy Deposit Photos*

Eliza and Stephen Jumel purchased Mount Morris in 1810 and rehabbed the battle-scarred property. Even though they frequently traveled to France, the couple spent their summers at the mansion. More than one year after her husband's death in 1832, Eliza got hitched to the former vice president of the United States, Aaron Burr. Yes, he's the man who fatally shot Alexander Hamilton during that infamous duel on July 11, 1804.

When asked if he had encountered Morris-Jumel's former matriarch in the Federal-style mansion, Davalos said, "Yes" without hesitation. "Eliza's spirit is all over this house," he told me, adding that the matriarch remained at her Manhattan mansion for the last six years of her life, dying there at age ninety in 1865.

Angela Artuso, the founder and director of the Gotham Paranormal Research Society, has investigated the mansion for more than five years and echoed Davalos's sentiments regarding the historic property's hauntings.

Based on her team's experiences investigating the haunted house, she believes Eliza Jumel had a strong personality and posthumously demands respect from the property's visitors. "She knew what she wanted and how to get it," Artuso explained. "She made the rules in the home and made sure no one deviated from any of them. I also feel the one person who truly had her heart was Stephen Jumel."

Artuso said Aaron Burr's room on the second floor "has a very odd energy to it" and seems to be a hotspot for paranormal activity. "We captured a voice screaming at us on video in Burr's room but could not tell if it was male or female," she said.

During an investigation in the former vice president's bed chambers, a member from Artuso's Gotham Paranormal Research Society team sang several songs from the Broadway musical *Hamilton* and their ghost-hunting equipment picked up a direct response to the tunes. "The odd thing about it was that the K2 meters pulsed to the rhythm of the songs, almost as if they were clapping along," Artuso said. "When the music stopped, so did the pulsing. Not sure if that was truly paranormal in nature but it was certainly interesting."

Artuso said the hallway on the second floor is particularly active, especially outside of the room of Jumel's grandson, William Chase. "I've had my hair touched and tugged there," Artuso explained. "I was gently pushed and nudged from behind as if someone was trying to say, 'get out of here and go away.' I've heard loud exhales and breathy sounds close to my face. It's almost as if there's someone standing guard and that's the feeling I get on that floor."

The veteran investigator also feels a presence at the entrance of the house near the staircase. "I always have the feeling that whoever enters the mansion is being closely watched and 'evaluated' for their approval," Artuso said.

The Brooklyn-based paranormal team had their most profound experience while investigating the Morris-Jumel Mansion's second floor. "We were spread out in Aaron Burr's bedroom and in the hallway. All of a sudden we started hearing our REM-Pods going off which were downstairs in the main hall at the bottom of the stairs," Artuso told me. "We heard loud footsteps that sounded like someone was walking around downstairs as well as coming up the steps but no one was there. All of our equipment was going off in the main hallway and would not stop. We had to actually stop the investigation to inspect the house and make sure no one broke into the mansion."

Both Davalos and Artuso believe the property is definitely one of the city's most haunted. Based on my baseline sweep of the historic structure, I have to agree.

Originally called Mount Morris, the Morris-Jumel Mansion is located in Manhattan's Washington Heights neighborhood. *Courtesy Deposit Photos*

After my spirited visit to the Morris-Jumel Mansion, I hopped on the subway's "A" train and headed downtown to Washington's other Revolutionary War–era hangout, Fraunces Tavern.

Originally built in 1719 as a residence, the structure was sold to Samuel Fraunces and was converted into "Queen's Head Tavern" in 1762. The watering hole became a hub for Manhattan's elite. Patrons established the city's first chamber of commerce in the building's Long Room in 1768.

The tavern quickly became a hotspot in the days leading up to the American Revolution. In fact, the Sons of Liberty and other groups plotted the lesser-known "New York Tea Party" in 1774 and gathered there to mobilize support for the rebels. When the Patriots commandeered the enemy's cannons in 1775 and fired at the redcoats, the British retaliated and sent a cannonball through the building's roof. Samuel Fraunces also passed on vital information to the American Patriots regarding General Benedict Arnold's traitorous acts.

George Washington was a regular at Fraunces Tavern. When the British evacuated New York City, the general and his officers celebrated their victory at the haunt located at 54 Pearl Street. The future president delivered his famous farewell address in 1783 there and he returned in 1789 to party once again after his inauguration at New York's Federal Hall.

Four years after selling the tavern in 1785, Samuel Fraunces became Washington's executive steward. The tavern's importance continued, even after the owner's departure, when the building hosted the Continental Congress. It also became the gathering spot for several newly created governmental agencies.

A series of fires ravaged the structure during the nineteenth century and Fraunces Tavern struggled for survival until the Sons of the Revolution set up shop there in 1883. The group ultimately purchased the historically significant building in 1904 and, three years later, converted it into a museum.

During my visit to Fraunces Tavern on the day after Halloween, I was blown away by the importance of the relics on display in the museum upstairs. Somehow, the Sons of Liberty secured one of George Washington's teeth and a lock of his hair. There's also a small piece of the dead president's coffin.

When I asked my tour guide if the museum still had the Bible used to swear in Washington as the nation's first commander-in-chief, he shook his head no. After the September 11 attacks in 2001, the book was removed from Fraunces Tavern and secured by the Freemasonry.

Walking into the museum's historic Long Room, you could almost hear the disembodied voices from America's patriotic past. My empathic abilities started to kick into high gear as soon as I stepped into the one room in the museum where you couldn't take photos.

I was able to make out a male voice or two, but the lingering residual energy sounded more like whispers than an actual audible conversation.

However, I did pick up what sounded like a female spirit speaking French. She was desperate to communicate with me. It sounded like she was saying "bonjour" coupled with an entire sentence I couldn't make out. One word I was able to understand with my basic French vocabulary was *meutre,* which means murder.

Shaken by the spirit's sadness, I asked the museum's guide if anybody was killed in the upstairs area and he said, "Yes." He also mentioned that Fraunces Tavern was bombed by the British in 1775 and 1975, and it was possible the casualties from those two disasters could have been what I was connecting to psychically.

My gut feeling, however, suggested that the mysterious female spirit had lived in the building and was killed during a domestic dispute.

According to the tour guide, Fraunces Tavern did have a blood stained past life as a boarding house. In 1798, a famous ballerina named Anna Gardie lived with her husband in the transient hotel. Originally from the French colony of Saint-Domingue, which was later renamed Haiti, Gardie found fame in France and eventually the United States during the late eighteenth century. In the early morning of July 21, 1798, she was fatally stabbed by her husband, whose subsequent suicide left behind an orphaned son.

After a brief-but-memorable visit to Fraunces Tavern, I walked to Manhattan's oldest public building in continuous use, St. Paul's Chapel, in search of the "presidential pew" frequented by Washington. He regularly prayed at the city's only colonial-era church still standing. It was his chapel of choice until the founding fathers relocated to Philadelphia in 1790.

I walked into the hallowed doors of St. Paul's, expecting to see a memorial of some sorts honoring Washington. Nope. The guards informed me that the "presidential pew" is no longer accessible to the general public. Disappointed I couldn't check out the spot

St. Paul's Chapel is nicknamed "The Little Chapel That Stood" and is the oldest surviving church building in Manhattan. *Courtesy Deposit Photos*

where Washington once prayed, I decided to walk through the church's graveyard outside.

For the record, I have an odd fascination with historic cemeteries. As the author of a dozen historical-based ghost books, I've spent many sleepless nights frolicking among the headstones in search of the skeletal secrets forgotten by history.

When it comes to paranormal investigations in cemeteries, my demonologist friend James Annitto told me they're perfect for beginners looking to learn the tricks of the trade. He said historic burial grounds may have "lots of contamination, but that's what makes you a great investigator and how you learn," he told me, adding that outdoor locations are difficult for the most experienced paranormal investigators because of false-positive readings on equipment because of noise, temperature fluctuations, and wind. "It gives you the ability to decipher what's contamination and what is plausible paranormal activity."

Armed with Annitto's advice, I decided to attempt communication with the spirits believed to still linger in the burial ground outside of St. Paul's Chapel. I whipped out my trusty dowsing rods, hoping to connect with Washington or the other ghosts associated with the American Revolution.

As soon as I questioned if there were any spirits in the cemetery, my "witch sticks" started to spin uncontrollably. Yes, the graveyard's ghosts wanted to communicate.

First, I asked if Washington's spirit was still there. No. I then mentioned Alexander Hamilton, hoping the Broadway musical based on the founding father was getting some traction in the afterlife. They crossed, indicating that the ghosts did know about the country's first president and the secretary of the treasury.

Finally, I asked the spirits to use the dowsing rods to point to their gravestone so I could ask more directed questions. What happened next moved me to tears. My copper rods pointed to the Bell of Hope in the courtyard right outside of the chapel's doors. I didn't realize its significance until I read the inscription: "Forged in adversity—11.September.2001."

The bell was a memorial for the victims of the World Trade Center attacks.

Known as the "Little Chapel That Stood," the Episcopal church became a haven for rescue workers in the days after the September 11 tragedy. Thousands of volunteers gathered at St. Paul's Chapel, serving meals and providing support. Because of its close proximity to Ground Zero, it's a miracle the building is still standing. The property survived without even a broken window.

Of course, this isn't the first time St. Paul's Chapel avoided tragedy. Days after the Continental Army left New York City in the hands of the British in September 1776, a massive fire broke out on Whitehall Street, destroying the rector's house and nearby Trinity Church.

While a bucket brigade was ordered to put out the fire that engulfed the chapel's roof in 1776, what happened 225 years later remains a mystery. During the 9/11 attacks, it's commonly believed that the church was protected by a giant sycamore tree planted in the graveyard. The spirits, however, had a different account. When I asked if they guarded the church in 2001, my L-shaped rods crossed quickly indicating a definitive yes.

I imagined the ghosts forming a shield of protection, guarding the sacred grounds of St. Paul's Chapel from the horrors that unfolded as the Twin Towers collapsed only 100 yards away.

Then I felt a familiar tingling sensation. *Something just passed through me,* I thought. There was a jolt of electricity and then I felt an overwhelming sense of peace. I was shivering in the beauty and the madness of the moment.

As I was communicating with the spirits of the cemetery, a white feather fell from the skies and landed right in front of me. I looked up. There were no birds perched in the trees or flying above. Are angels protecting the "Little Chapel That Stood" on Broadway? My dowsing rods crossed. Yes.

I held my breath.

TOWN CRIER PROFILE: BRIAN J. CANO

*War is hell. It wasn't a great time and I couldn't imagine any of
the people living it felt like they were going to be celebrated in the
future.*

—Brian J. Cano, *Paranormal Caught on Camera*

Brian J. Cano, a featured investigator on television shows such as
Haunted Collector and *Paranormal Caught on Camera*, is surrounded by the ghosts of the American Revolution.

He also has something in common with the nation's first president.

"George Washington and I share a birthday," Cano told me in
a recent interview. "We were both born on February 22nd. I was
president of the student council, but that's about as far as the
comparisons go."

As a native of New York's Staten Island, Cano was a stone's
throw to the historic and haunted locations associated with the
American War of Independence. "During the Revolution, Staten
Island was a Loyalist stronghold," he said. "I'm not big on numer-
ology, but on September 11, 1776, there was a conference held
here with British Admiral Richard Howe and Benjamin Franklin,
John Adams, and a couple of other Patriots."

Photo courtesy Brian J. Cano

Cano admits there's some interesting Revolutionary War history in his own backyard.

"The British and the Patriots met on the tip of Staten Island at a location now known as the Conference House," he said. "They were trying to avert the war and made an attempt to come up with some agreement to avoid a long, drawn-out war. But it didn't happen."

Built by Captain Christopher Billopp sometime before 1680, the Conference House is believed to have some lingering energy associated with the events that unfolded during what was called the Staten Island Peace Conference. "There's a lot on Staten Island in general in regard to paranormal activity, but when it comes to the Conference House, most of the things reported there have ties to the Revolutionary War era," Cano told me. "People claim seeing redcoat soldiers marching the grounds. There was a Native American burial ground next to the property, so there are some additional energies associated with the land."

Cano said there's an unverified legend associated with the Conference House suggesting that the previous owner murdered someone by throwing her down the stairs. "People report seeing a woman looking out of the window and walking the grounds," Cano said, adding that he first investigated the Conference House in 2004. "What I hear over and over again is there was crying and screaming from the murdered woman's spirit."

When asked if there is any historical documentation to back up the female haunting the Conference House, Cano told me the story is unsubstantiated. He's not even sure if the victim was the owner's wife or if she was enslaved. "It varies depending on who you ask," he said. "Some say she was the woman of the house and some say she was a servant."

Armed with more than two decades of experience in the paranormal, Cano's initial plan was to investigate haunted locations close to home. However, he encountered some red tape along the way.

"My personal experience with the historic locations in New York City is that they are a hard nut to crack," he said. "Depending on which side of the door you're on, an investigation opens it up to liability and things they didn't expect like a group claiming there's a demon or something dark lurking in the shadows. These sort of over-the-top claims would deeply impact the historical significance and reputation of the property. There's a reason why many of these locations are gun shy about allowing in paranormal investigators."

Cano said if heritage organizations are selective about the groups they let in to investigate and keep an open mind, it could be an extremely positive experience. "The investigators may be able to fill in the blanks and move the history of the location forward," he explained.

When asked if he believes the ghosts associated with the American Revolution are more residual or intelligent in nature, Cano said it's a case-by-case scenario. "In general, I find they're more residual," he said. "Nobody is interacting with these residual redcoats and playback spirits. They're just observing them and reporting what they've seen. If the spirits are not responding, then I feel like they're definitely residual."

According to Cano's theory regarding residual hauntings, they may have an expiration date. "I believe, over time, we're going to see less and less of the residual spirits," he told me. "If you think about it, radioactive isotopes have a half-life and the energy will eventually subside. With that science in mind, I believe these residual energies can only persist for so long unless they are somehow re-energized."

Would this explain the lack of modern sightings of Revolutionary War—era spirits? "We're talking about a specific era in time," he said. "No one is talking to ghosts from the Dark Ages or to cave man ghosts."

Certain locations, however, will continue to "re-energize" their residual hauntings thanks to period re-enactors and a continued remembrance of the events that shaped our nation. Cano cited Boston's historic North End neighborhood as an example of a significant Revolutionary War—era location that continues to be a fertile environment for modern hauntings.

"I haven't spent a lot of time in Boston, but I remember looking around in the old North End section of the city and walking from the hotel to the set every day," he said, recalling an experience he had while investigating a cigar bar on Hanover Street for the *Haunted Collector* television show. "I kept thinking these were the same paths some really influential people walked in the past. Hundreds of years ago, important things were happening in Boston."

Stanza dei Sigari made front-page news in March 2013 when the subterranean cigar parlor was investigated by Cano and the team from *Haunted Collector*. According to the *Boston Herald*, manager David Riccio Jr. wasn't just blowing smoke when it came to reported paranormal phenomena.

He sent in a video tape to the show's producers stating that some of his customers and employees had been scared off by unexplainable activity experienced at his cigar bar.

"There's more than just smoke wafting through the air at Stanza dei Sigari," the *Herald* reported. "The North End cigar bar's workers are blaming a paranormal presence for broken shelves, flashing lights and unexplained bumps in the night in the basement shop on Hanover Street."

Riccio said his family-owned business has a history of paranormal activity. "I've always, even when I was a kid, thought there were ghosts down there," he said.

The manager said employees witnessed plates flying off tables and lights turning on and off. A terrified waitress claimed someone, or something, was standing behind her one night. When she turned around, she spotted a black shadow dart across the room and then escaped through a glass door.

Cano, the crew's tech manager and second in command on *Haunted Collector* program, wrote in an online blog post in 2013 that he was smitten with the location. "There is so much famous history in Boston and especially the North End, where our case was located. Honestly, I was surprised about the layout of this part of town," Cano wrote on his behind-the-scenes blog. "I found it to be very European, with thin, winding side streets barely wide enough for a single car, bistros, bakeries, and bike riders everywhere. The chain stores and restaurants I was used to seeing were nowhere to be found and that was strangely comforting. Corny as it sounds, I really could feel the echoes of the past reverberating off of every brick in the road, every tree that swayed in the wind."

John Zaffis, a legend in the paranormal scene and nephew of the late Ed and Lorraine Warren, led the *Haunted Collector* investigation with Cano at Stanzi dei Sigari. His team's findings were shocking.

The building was built in 1896 and the land was formerly home to a "baby farm," a Victorian-era underground business, which, in exchange for cash, took children from parents who were unable to care for them.

Riccio was born in the building located at 292 Hanover Street and heard various tales from his father and grandfather about the structure's history, but he was shocked to learn about the sordid details involving children. "We were freaked out, it was a baby farm," he told the *Boston Herald*. In addition to kids being sold at the North End building, some of them were also killed.

The baby farm was owned and operated by a woman named Miss Elwood who had a history of abusing babies left at the baby farm. According to research uncovered by the TV show, she may have killed a few of the orphaned infants using arsenic. Cano and the *Haunted Collector* crew found a medical kit containing an 1870s-era syringe hidden within the building's foundation.

Cano said the team spent days canvassing the location, ruling out other logical explanations for the paranormal phenomena, before they stumbled upon the nineteenth century baby farm arti-fact. "At the cafe, we checked out the reports of cups and dishes flying off the shelves, the spinning wheel of the coffee grinder as well as the tommy gun encased above the back steps," Cano wrote. "There was so much to see and so much to check off the list there."

Once Zaffis removed the Victorian-era medical kit, the haunt-ings at Stanza dei Sigari reportedly stopped.

Cano told me the residual energy associated with the North End Cigar bar is a perfect example of the spirits of '76 taking a backseat to more modern paranormal activity. "As we go on in time, the ghosts from the Revolutionary War will dissipate and we'll start talking to ghosts from the twentieth century," he said. "As we move forward in our timeline, the energy also moves forward."

When it comes to spirit communication with the founding fathers associated with the American Revolution, Cano isn't con-vinced they're still sticking around. "The minute you start inves-tigating, you're sending a signal to the astral plane that you're attempting to make contact with the spirit realm," he said. "When we send out that signal, you never know who or what is responding."

If investigators claim they're communicating with the spirit of George Washington or Benjamin Franklin, for example, Cano said it may be wishful thinking. "If someone is trying to contact George Washington and they get a response, they're going to automati-cally think it's him," he said. "How would they know what George Washington sounded like? There's no logic behind that approach. People try to connect the dots too quickly."

As someone who shares a birthday with America's first president, Cano said Washington probably powered through most of his legendary career and probably doesn't want to revisit the blood-stained battlefields he once overlooked. "He didn't want to do half of the things he did during his lifetime, but he did it because it was required of him. He did it out of service," Cano said. "He put one foot in front of the other and kept walking. He had no inkling there would be monuments honoring him one day or that he would be on the one-dollar bill."

When it comes to the founding fathers, Cano said we put them on pedestals, but they were regular people who happened to win the battle for independence and probably wouldn't want to relive the day-to-day stresses of creating a new nation.

"War is hell," he said. "It wasn't a great time and I couldn't imagine any of the people living it felt like they were going to be celebrated in the future. When people look back at events like the American Revolution, what actually took place is probably very different from the romanticized story we now commemorate."

THE PATRIOTS

During the American Revolution, the Liberty Bell in Philadelphia, Pennsylvania, was hidden in a church sixty miles away to prevent the British from melting it down to musket balls. *Courtesy Deposit Photos*

BENJAMIN
FRANKLIN

Years ago when I first started giving ghost tours in Boston, I spotted a Benjamin Franklin look-alike walking through Boston Common late one night in October. He was heading toward the gold-domed Massachusetts State House and seemed to be in a hurry. When I looked again, he was gone.

I initially shrugged it off as the Freedom Trail tour guide known to dress in Franklin-esque garb until I was contacted by a reader from Utah in July 2013 who visited the city's Granary Burial Ground on Tremont Street. The woman, who wishes to remain anonymous, swears she had a face-to-face encounter with the legendary founding father.

"When I was in Boston, I saw the ghost of Benjamin Franklin walk through the cemetery," the woman told me via email. "At first I thought it must be a reenactor, and I thought it was strange because it was at 10:00 p.m. and he was alone. Then I noticed he was all gray looking and looked exactly like the real Benjamin Franklin. As soon as I told my friends to look, he was gone," she wrote.

After doing some digging, it turns out Franklin's family is buried in Granary Burial Ground. There was an attempt to rename the cemetery dating back to 1660 the "Franklin Cemetery" in honor of the founding father's family, but the effort was dismissed in May 1830. Of course, many of the big names of the American Revolution are buried in Granary including Paul Revere, Samuel Adams, and the five victims of the Boston Massacre. There are reports that Revere's ghost, sometimes upon the horse on which he made his famous midnight ride, appears near his gravestone.

But no Franklin. Maybe his ghost was merely visiting his family plot in the afterlife?

My quest to find the spirit of the country's first postmaster general led me to Philadelphia, Pennsylvania. On a whim, I headed to the "City of Brotherly Love" one chilly weekend in November 2019. After visiting many of the historic sites synonymous with the bespectacled founding father and chatting with several Philadelphians, I was told Franklin's spirit has been spotted all over the city.

Yes, his ghost apparently gets around.

My first stop was Christ Church Burial Ground with a history dating back to 1719. The graveyard is the final resting place for several signers of the Declaration of Independence including Joseph Hewes, Francis Hopkinson, George Ross, and Benjamin Rush. Franklin and his wife Deborah were also interred at the cemetery, which attracts around a hundred thousand tourists each year.

I chatted with two docents manning the information booth at the burial ground's entrance. When I asked the volunteers if Franklin's spirit had been spotted around his memorial, they both nodded. A psychic-medium picked up on his lingering energy after standing over the inventor's grave marker.

The docents were told by the psychic that Franklin appears as a "golden butterfly" in spirit form. The color of the winged insect represents a new life, a transformation, or a rebirth. While I didn't encounter his ghost or even a butterfly that chilly afternoon at Christ Church Burial Ground, I did leave a penny at his gravesite honoring the old Philadelphia tradition.

As I was placing the coin at the memorial, I was told by one of the volunteers that his famous *bon mot* has been twisted over time. A penny saved is a penny earned? Not exactly. Franklin actually wrote, "a penny saved is two pence clear" in *Poor Richard's Almanack*.

After leaving the cemetery, I headed to his other postmortem hangout, the American Philosophical Society's library, which he founded in 1743. The building is literally across the street from Independence Hall. According to local legend, there's a statue of Franklin that supposedly animates and dances around. In 1844 a cleaning lady reportedly spotted his ghostly specter in the library and he also has been seen sitting on the historic structure's granite steps.

His spirit also regularly visits Independence Hall, according to several park rangers, where he's seen reading a scrolled-up document. His apparition is always accompanied by a mysterious mist.

During my first evening in Philadelphia, I spent a few hours on a bench behind the library hoping to see Franklin's statue come to life. I must admit, the downtown area is extremely creepy at night. In fact, I heard what sounded like footsteps behind me on the cobblestones, but nobody was there.

Somewhat freaked out, I crossed Chestnut Street and noticed a sign advertising the Benjamin Franklin Museum. In an attempt to connect with his spirit on a deeper level, I walked down the alley to the steel "ghost house," which was the foundational ruins of his former home. As I looked through the plexiglass display peeking at what was his basement, I noticed a well and it took me a moment to realize it was Franklin' privy (an old-school term for toilet).

There was a man standing behind me, or so I thought, and he jokingly said, "that's where George Washington [relieved himself]." To be frank, the mystery man's comments were too crass to repeat.

I laughed and quickly turned around. The only person in the area behind me was a tourist briskly walking by the museum. He had earbuds on and was listening to music. I don't think he made the off-color joke.

Was it Franklin? Yes, I'm convinced. The founding father definitely had a penchant for toilet humor. And, based on the hilarious one-liner coming from what seemed to be a disembodied voice, Franklin has a potty mouth in the afterlife.

FRANKLIN'S HAUNT: BOSTON LIGHT

BOSTON HARBOR, MA—There's an inexplicable mystique radiating from Little Brewster's Boston Light. Armed with more than three centuries of maritime history, it's located approximately nine miles offshore from downtown and dates back to 1716.

Boston Light was rebuilt in the eighteenth century after the redcoats torched the original structure during the Revolutionary War. It's the second-oldest working lighthouse in the country, and its ninety-eight-foot-high tower has seen almost three centuries of tragedy, starting with the death of the light's first keeper, George Worthylake, who drowned alongside his wife, daughter, and two other men when their boat capsized a few feet from the island's rocky terrain in 1718.

The ghosts from the Boston Light's early days have captivated the imagination of the city's land-bound inhabitants for years. A young Benjamin Franklin, then an up-and-coming printer, penned a ballad about the Worthylake incident called "Lighthouse Tragedy," which he later dismissed as "wretched stuff" but joked that it "sold prodigiously." Boston Light's second keeper, Robert Saunders, met a similar fate and drowned only a few days after taking the job. The tower, which originally stood at seventy-five feet, caught fire in 1751, and the building was damaged so intensely that only the walls remained. The British, angry that the colonists had tried to disengage the beacon during the Revolution, apparently destroyed Boston Light in 1776 while heading out of the Boston Harbor. It was rebuilt in 1783 but witnessed several more tragedies, including two shipwrecks, the *Miranda* in 1861 and the *Calvin F. Baker* in 1898, which resulted in three crewmen freezing to death in the rigging.

In addition to the onslaught of natural disaster, one keeper in 1844 set up a "Spanish" cigar factory, carting in young girls from Boston and claiming the stogies sold in the city were foreign imports. Captain Tobias Cook's clandestine cigar business was quickly fingered as fraudulent and shut down.

President John F. Kennedy legislated that the Boston Light would be the last manned lighthouse in the country. It has been inhabited for almost three centuries, even when the tower was automated in 1998. One island mystery, known as the Ghost Walk, refers to a stretch of water several miles east of the lighthouse where the warning sounds from the tower's larger-than-life foghorn cannot be heard by passing ships. For years, no one has been able to scientifically explain the so-called Ghost Walk's absence of sound, not even a crew of MIT students sent in the mid-1970s to spend an entire summer on the island but who were still unable to crack the case.

However, talk of the paranormal has trumped the island's Ghost Walk mystery. "It has withstood blizzards, erosion, fires, lightning, shipwrecks and ghosts," mused a report in the April 29, 1999, edition of the

Boston Globe, which profiled Little Brewster's Chris Sutherland from the U.S. Coast Guard. Apparently, the petty officer noticed tiny human footprints in the snow while keeping the light in the late '90s. "I'm not saying it's a ghost," he said, "but I don't know. In the past, there were kids out here, lightkeepers' families. There were shipwrecks along the rocks."

A former Coast Guard engineer who lived on the island in the late 1980s, David Sandrelli, told the *Globe* there have been reports of a lady walking down the stairs. Also, he said crew members stationed on Little Brewster would hear weird noises in the night but would dismiss them, saying, "It's just George," an allusion to the ghosts from the Worthylake tragedy.

Sally Snowman, who was the first female keeper at the last occupied lighthouse in the country, told the *Globe* in 2003 that she had a few "just George" moments during her stint on Little Brewster. "I won't say if I believe or don't believe in any ghosts on the island," she said. "Let's just say I've heard plenty of stories. Some strange things do happen out here, like the fog signal, which works on reading moisture in the air, going off at 3:00 a.m. on a star-filled night. That's fun because you have to walk across the island to shut that sucker off. That can be weird."

Little Brewster's mascot, the black Labrador Sammy, reportedly had a close encounter in 1999. "He would stand up, run out of the room for no reason and was shaking all over," recalled a former keeper, Gary Fleming. "It really does get spooky. You have plenty of time here, and if you let your mind go, you can freak yourself out," Fleming said, adding that he believes in the supernatural.

Snowman echoed Fleming's comments about the canine mascot's odd nightly ritual. "He's been out here six years, and at dusk every night he barks and barks," she mused. "We call it the Shadwell Hour, after the slave who died."

So who's Shadwell? Mazzie B. Anderson, a woman who was stationed with her husband on Little Brewster in 1947, recalled hearing footsteps when no one was there and watching the foghorn engines magically start themselves when her husband was ill. She also heard maniacal laughter followed by the sobs of a female voice yelling, "Shaaaadwell, Shaaaadwell!" It turns out Worthylake, his wife, and their youngest daughter Ruth capsized near the island, and the oldest daughter, who was left behind with her friend Mary Thompson, reportedly witnessed her family's demise. In addition to servant George Cutler and friend John Edge, the capsized vessel included an enslaved African-American man.

According to lighthouse historian Jeremy D'Entremont, another person, rarely mentioned in the history books, was on the island that day. "The first keeper, George Worthylake, died in November 1718 along with five other people when their canoe capsized," he said. "One of the people who died was the slave. It's not necessarily well known that there were two slaves at Boston Light at that time—there was also a woman named Dinah."

Some believe the postmortem screams heard on the island belong to the forgotten African-American woman who watched the horror unfold off the shore of Little Brewster. "Somehow the canoe capsized and all went overboard," wrote Anderson in the October 1998 edition of *Yankee* magazine. "The African made a valiant attempt to save all hands but failed. The young girl was the last to go under, still calling his name. No one survived."

The name of the courageous African-American slave? He was known as Shadwell

SPIRITS OF '76: GALLOPING GHOSTS

I believe the Native American and animal bond most assuredly transcends the physical world.

—Gare Allen, *Ghost Crimes*

Gare Allen, a Florida-based author armed with more than a dozen paranormal-themed books, is my usual go-to expert when it comes to animal spirits. During the research phase of *Ghosts of the American Revolution*, I noticed a recurring theme with the paranormal activity I encountered along the way: *phantom equus caballus.*

Yes, ghost horses. I trotted over to Allen for advice.

"It doesn't surprise me when someone shares their encounter with the spirit of an animal, especially those we formed a bond with during their corporeal lives," Allen said. "Pets are often considered members of the family and their loss can be just as devastating as that of a human loved one."

Galloping ghosts? Allen told me the phenomenon is usually tied to their two-legged counterparts.

"The soldier-horse relationship during wartime must have been complex given the dangerous conditions," he explained. "Their mutual safety was quite dependent on each other's cooperation and inherent will to survive. The soldier's commitment to the horse's needs of food, water, and treatment of injuries undoubtedly fostered trust and loyalty. Similarly, a soldier's life literally rested on the strength of his stallion's back."

Allen believes the soldiers and horses developed a bond while navigating the life-and-death dangers of the Revolutionary War. "Action and instinct had to become one as did the desire to survive," he said. "As with human ghosts, perhaps the sightings of horse spirits on the battlefields of our past can be explained in the same fashion. Some searching for their former riders, some trapped between worlds, and others could be a harsh imprint of suffering so haunting it stamped itself in time."

This sort of psychic imprint or residual haunting has also been reported at the Old South Meeting House in Boston. Giddyup?

There's an eerie silence when one opens the hallowed white doors and walks into this important Revolutionary War–era structure. Inside, visitors can see where Benjamin Franklin was baptized and, more importantly, where Samuel Adams fueled the whole "no taxation without representation" Patriot war cry against British rule.

The Boston Tea Party rally was originally slated for Faneuil Hall, but it was moved to the Old South Meeting House because it was large enough to handle the spill-over masses. At the time, it was the largest building in colonial Boston. Old South was also where thousands of outraged Bostonians gathered to protest the Boston Massacre in March 1770, in which five colonists were killed by British soldiers.

Built in 1729 by a Puritan congregation who probably had no idea this Freedom Trail favorite would play such an important role in American history as the go-to gathering place of record for more than three centuries, the Old South Meeting House is also reportedly haunted.

Michael Baker, investigator with Para-Boston, organized a paranormal investigation at the historic building. Their findings? The paranormal investigation team did record an EVP (electromagnetic voice phenomenon) of a male voice saying, "Who's there?" There were also first-hand accounts of chains rattling in the lower area of the meeting house and a bizarre recording anomaly coming from the building's steeple.

Was any evidence discovered of a Revolutionary War–era horse spirit lingering in the building, as some have suggested? Naay . . . or should that be "neighhhh." Unless the EVP was of a dead Mr. Ed. However, several visitors to the building have reported smelling hay and one woman who tied the knot in the Old South Meeting House said she had a close encounter with the horse spirit.

For the record, the redcoats ransacked the building during the Revolutionary War and used it as a horse stable and riding school for British soldiers. George Washington walked by the building during the late 1700s and was extremely unhappy with how the Brits had desecrated this important landmark. Whoa, Nellie.

In addition to the reports of ghost horses at Old South Meeting House, there are accounts of a spectral stallion roaming the coastline of Peddocks Island in Boston Harbor.

The mysterious outer harbor island made a cameo in the opening sequence of Martin Scorsese's film *Shutter Island.* While the novel written by Dennis Lehane was inspired by the campus of brick buildings on Long Island, exterior scenes for the made-in-Massachusetts movie were actually shot on the 184-acre series of interconnected drumlins.

And, yes, Peddocks Island is as creepy as it looks on film.

When the film's protagonist Teddy Daniels, played by Leonardo DiCaprio, approaches the fictional Shutter Island by boat, he's greeted by two armed guards who quickly whisk him away into the bowels of the Ashecliffe Hospital for the Criminally Insane. Daniels passes by the weathered brick buildings of Peddocks Island's Fort Andrews, a World War II–era fort replete with ivy-covered walls and penitentiary-style ruins. At one point, there were twenty-six buildings on the island, including a guardhouse, a stable, prisoner barracks, and a fire station.

Today, only one dozen or so buildings from Fort Andrews remain. The rest, active since 1904 through World War II, were destroyed in 2011 after filming the movie. The Department of Recreation and Conservation (DCR) has painstakingly restored the structures still standing. In fact, the DCR recently rehabbed the 1940s-era chapel, which was originally built from a military kit, and created a series of cabins, known as yurts, for enthusiasts wanting to spend the night on the creepy backdrop for *Shutter Island.*

Many of the visitors who camp on Peddocks Island claim it's Boston Harbor's most haunted.

Jerry McCormack, a Massachusetts State Park Ranger, told the *American-Statesman* he had his most profound paranormal experience as a child while roaming the prisoner-of-war barracks on Peddocks Island. "Because his father was the site supervisor for several of Boston Harbor's most haunted islands, McCormack and his siblings had free rein to roam and explore places like Fort Andrews on Peddocks Island after dark," reported the *Statesman.* "It was there, at age ten, that McCormack says he had his first ghostly encounter. Wandering at night near deserted barracks that once housed Italian prisoners of war, Jerry and his family heard the clear, soulful sounds of a piano sonata wafting through the air."

McCormack said, "The piano man has been tapping out music since he was a prisoner here during World War II. He died trying to escape the island by swimming off it, returning for eternal night-time encores."

The park ranger was also mysteriously tapped on the back by an unseen force while exploring the dark hallway on Georges Island. When asked if he believed in the paranormal, McCormack responded: "You betcha. This is Boston."

Battalions of troops trained at Fort Andrews during World War I, and thousands of Italian soldiers stayed on Peddocks Island in a prisoner-of-war camp during World War II. They were detained in North Africa in 1943 following Mussolini's surrender to the Allied forces. The prison was not overly strict and the POWs were given weekend passes to the North End where they romanced local girls and enjoyed home-cooked dinners.

Matilda Silvia, a lifelong resident of Peddocks Island, wrote about the foreign gentlemen she interacted with in the 1940s in her memoir, *Once Upon an Island.* "On weekends, they rotated on a two-day pass to Boston. One group alternated each weekend from Friday night until Sunday night," Silvia wrote. Those remaining on the island were allowed to have friends and relatives visit them on either day of the weekend. The guests were not allowed to stay overnight."

The POWs were sent back to Italy in September 1945. Many survivors of the camp said their stay in America felt more like a vacation and less like an internment. Silvia didn't recall any soldier trying to escape the island. However, there were at least three reported deaths in the twentieth century. In 1906, two soldiers capsized and drowned while paddling to Georges from Peddocks. In 1934, another serviceman died on Peddocks because of the harsh New England elements. He reportedly froze to death and his remains were shipped to Nantasket.

Another mysterious death took place in 2012. A thirty-five-year-old man was on the island during the off-season and sustained head injuries after jumping on an elevator platform and then going into cardiac arrest. First responders found his lifeless body in the basement of the quartermaster building. The DCR employee on duty apparently invited a group of friends to the island and they were drinking alcohol. "The caretakers are there to protect the investment we've made on the island and to ward off any vandals—and we do have a history of vandalism on Peddocks Island," said DCR spokesperson S.J. Port. The DCR caretaker was placed on unpaid administrative leave. The death was ruled accidental.

So, who was the piano man? Several volunteers and employees who have spent time on the island were interviewed for this book. One volunteer, who asked to remain anonymous, said he'd seen the actual piano played by the supposed ghost of Peddocks Island. "It was in one of the off-limits prisoner-of-war barracks," he said.

"I also remember seeing an amazing mural painted on the walls in the prison. It looked like something you would see in Italy. It's all boarded up now and you can't go inside to see it, but I remember sneaking in one night because I heard rumors that one of the Italian prisoners painted it. The mural was beautiful."

For the record, the barracks are now completely off-limits since the accidental death in 2012.

Campers who frequented Peddocks often talked about hearing piano music on the island. Other reports said the music from beyond sounded more like wind chimes. Campers also talked about spotting a greyish-colored horse galloping on the island and disappearing without a trace.

Is there also a ghost horse on Peddocks? One man said he calls the spirit animal "Smokey" and affirmed the horse has been spotted on the island for years. Volunteers who helped rehabilitate the structures on Peddocks swear the stable, which served as overnight quarters for park rangers and DCR employees who weren't staying in the renovated old guardhouse, is the most haunted structure on Peddocks. They've reported hearing noises, as if a horse was tapping its hoof, and the smell of hay, even though the island has been without a horse for years.

"I've seen Smokey several times," insisted one volunteer. "He would gallop across the shoreline and then disappear, like a puff of smoke, when our boat approached the island."

Named after Leonard Peddock, who may or may not have actually lived on his namesake land, the island has a history of animals grazing its mainland. In fact, before the Revolution in the summer of 1775, the British looted the island. They stole sheep and cattle from Peddocks and reportedly burned down buildings and farms on Thompson and Grape. They even stole two horses from Governors Island, which is now the runway area for Logan International Airport in East Boston.

Maybe the ghost horse is related to the hell-raising redcoats during the Revolution?

Another possible explanation relates to a tragedy involving Native Americans and a crew of French explorers on Peddocks Island years before the Puritans established Boston in 1630. "A French trading vessel was riding anchor off the shores of the island when the Indians massacred all the men except five whom they saved to exhibit around to the various tribes of Massachusetts," wrote Edward Rowe Snow in *The Islands of Boston Harbor*. Snow also alluded to the possibility that a colonial-era French encampment was set up on the East Head of the island, the future location of Fort Andrews.

Cursed Native American land stained with blood? According to Allen, it's definitely a viable explanation. But he strongly believes it's something more sublime.

"Native Americans seem to have a significant spiritual relationship with animals," he explained. "Their reverence for some animals positioned them as lifetime guides, both in the physical world and after. The horse is seen as a strong symbol of freedom, citing mobility, strength, and great power. The horse also signified loyalty, love, and devotion. The equine species made this a literal gift, as their presence allowed Native Americans to use them for travel, hunting, and warfare."

Allen told me the ghost horse known as "Smokey" could be a sentinel spirit guarding Peddocks Island. "I believe the Native American and animal bond most assuredly transcends the physical world," he said.

GEORGE
WASHINGTON

While there's no denying our first president's heroics during the American Revolution, it's important to note that the legendary life of George Washington was full of contradictions.

Two decades after he was denied a British officer's rank, he became the commander-in-chief of an army in revolt against an empire he once served. Even though he had no desire to lead the country he protected during the War of Independence, Washington begrudgingly served two terms as president of the United States. While he emancipated the enslaved men and women, including his manservant William "Billy" Lee who stood by the leader's side during the battles that helped forge a nation, Washington was a slave owner most of his life.

The iconic leader also had an oddly antithetical relationship with religion. While he encouraged his fellow Americans to gather for worship services, he regularly didn't go to church. Washington served as an Anglican church vestryman and warden for fifteen years, but he would conveniently leave before actually taking communion. The founding father was an active member of the Freemasonry and seemed to be a very spiritual person, however, he never mentioned God in his writings and opted for the word *Providence* when referring to a higher power.

Would someone who appeared to have a cagey relationship with organized religion stick around in the afterlife? Author and paranormal researcher Joni Mayhan believes it's a viable possibility.

"At the time of death, I believe we have a choice to make," Mayhan told me. "We can either go through the white light to continue our spiritual journey, or we can stay where we are without a body. The reasons why people remain earthbound are as varied as the personalities of the people themselves. Some might stay to look over loved ones or to protect businesses or homes they loved. Others could have unfinished business or feel guilt from something they did while they were alive."

Mayhan said Washington's conflicting views on spirituality could result in an earthbound haunting. "Considering Washington's relationship with God, I believe it makes perfect sense he would dismiss the white light, seeing it as something that didn't interest him, and decide to remain on our physical plane of existence."

Washington's spirit has been spotted at the scene of his death in Mount Vernon and near the tomb where he's buried in Virginia. His ghost has also been seen at Woodlawn Plantation, which he gifted to his nephew Lawrence Lewis in 1799.

Similar to the ghosts of his colleague Benjamin Franklin, Washington's spirit gets around. "Like others who remain earthbound, Washington has free will and can move on to his afterlife any time he chooses," Mayhan said. "Judging by the various sightings, it appears he's quite content where he is, visiting all the places he enjoyed when he was alive."

His spirit was also spotted at least twice by soldiers during the Civil War's bloodiest battle in Gettysburg. The accounts portray Washington's ghost wearing a full uniform, riding a white horse, and leading Union soldiers to victory.

Michelle Hamilton, manager of the Mary Washington House, said it makes sense the spirit of America's first commander-in-chief participated in the pivotal Battle of Gettysburg. "I believe he comes back to check up on the country he helped create," she told me.

Hamilton said the spirits of both Washington and his wife Martha are seen at Mount Vernon, the first president's palatial estate situated on the banks of the Potomac River in Virginia. "Mount Vernon is such a beautiful place so I'm sure he has visited his final resting place," she said. "There are legends that Martha Washington has also been seen in the gardens. She also loved Mount Vernon, so that doesn't surprise me."

The tragic way Washington died at Mount Vernon, Hamilton said, could have resulted in a residual haunting. "He took a chill after being caught in an ice storm," she said. "He should have changed his clothing, but the Washingtons had guests and he didn't want to delay dinner."

Washington was supervising farm work on his property on December 12 and it began to snow. He didn't change out of his wet clothes once he returned home and headed straight to dinner. The following morning Washington had a sore throat. After a series of medical treatments that included blood-letting, he passed later in the evening of December 14, 1799.

His last request was to be buried three days after he died. "Have me decently buried; and do not let my body be put into the vault in less than three days after I am dead," he reportedly told his secretary, Tobias Lear. Apparently, it was a common fear to be interred too soon during the eighteenth century. Like many of his contemporaries, he was afraid to be buried alive.

After his death, Martha had their second-floor master bedroom at Mount Vernon sealed shut. She moved her sleeping quarters to the third floor. Why? According to Charles Stansfield's *Haunted Presidents*, Washington's spirit returned and his wife wanted to give him some space. "She had seen him, sitting up in bed, studying state papers and reports of national and international events," Stansfield wrote. "Was she afraid of her husband's ghost? 'Oh no,' she is said to have replied. 'It is just that he needs his quiet time to ponder the nation's fate.' Martha knew to give her husband solitude when he confronted the pressing problems of leadership."

Stansfield wrote that Washington regularly returns to the tomb where he and his wife are buried. "Washington's phantom is said to appear as a misty figure, glowing slightly with a greenish phosphorescence," he wrote in *Haunted Presidents*. "Supposedly, he is most likely to appear near the anniversary of his own death, December 14, and that of Martha's death, March 22."

Apparently, Washington's ghost has a calendar. It's also said his spirit leaves a bouquet of red roses near his wife's final resting place. This postmortem gesture makes sense because Martha loyally supported her husband throughout the American Revolution, including the notoriously brutal winter at Valley Forge.

There's no denying the love Washington felt for his wife and the sentiment continues in the afterlife.

WASHINGTON'S HAUNT: WADSWORTH HOUSE

CAMBRIDGE, MA—Built in 1726, the Early-Georgian Wadsworth House at Harvard University is one of the few large houses not constructed by a Tory. Facing Massachusetts Avenue and an architectural anomaly of sorts thanks to its five-bay façade and simplistic colonial design, Wadsworth House served as the primary residence for the president of Harvard until 1849. Over the years, the house would host visiting ministers and student boarders including Ralph Waldo Emerson. The second-oldest surviving structure on Harvard's campus, the historic building lost its front yard when Massachusetts Avenue was widened.

Wadsworth House was also a major player in the days leading up to the Revolutionary War. The fight for independence began on April 19, 1775, and thousands of armed men from all over New England gathered in Cambridge. However, there was a housing shortage. Soldiers camped in the Cambridge Common while Harvard, responding to the growing anti-Tory sentiment and concerned about student safety, canceled classes on May 1 and allowed displaced soldiers to set up temporary shelter in its buildings. Oddly, classes took a wartime field trip nearly twenty miles away in Concord when schoolwork resumed on October 5.

On June 15, 1775, the Continental Congress appointed George Washington as commander-in-chief of the army, and he assumed his role as the leader of the troops on July 3, 1775. Washington set up his first headquarters at Wadsworth House, located at 1341 Massachusetts Avenue, and it's said he hashed out plans to oust King George from Boston in the historic landmark's parlor room. Washington, who remained in Cambridge until April 1776, later moved into his primary residence located at the Longfellow House on Brattle Street. Apparently, Wadsworth was in complete disrepair at the time.

In addition to its role in the Revolutionary War, there are several reports of Washington-era residual hauntings that continue to linger in the chambers of the old-school haunt. "One account explains that early one morning, forty years ago, a cleaning lady vacuuming alone in Wadsworth House saw a grim character in a tricorn hat and cloak silently come down the stairs and go out the door," reports the *Harvard Crimson* in 1997. The reporter, however, never confirmed the rumor, adding that "none of the staff at the Wadsworth House have heard anything about a man in a tricorn hat."

An article dating back to 1986 confirmed a similar story. "Over at Wadsworth House, where Washington once slept, ghosts of American Patriots wearing tricorn hats and cloaks have not haunted the colonial building in at least twenty-five years," the *Crimson* added.

There was a report from a Harvard employee, however, who worked in the Wadsworth House that would suggest the historic building's ghosts are still lurking in the shadows. Clark Schuler, a tech specialist, came into his office early one winter morning and had what he believed was a ghostly encounter in 2014.

"I was the only one in the building, in the downstairs offices, with the door right behind me," Schuler told Sarah Sweeney at the *Harvard Gazette*. "But I felt like someone was there. And I heard someone clear his throat, and I spun around thinking, 'How'd you get in here?' The door was right there. If someone had been standing there, I would've bumped right into him."

Spirits wearing tricorn hats? Yep, Harvard Square has them. For the record, a residual haunting isn't technically a ghost but a playback or recording of a past event. Based on the so-called Stone Tape theory, apparitions aren't intelligent spirits that interact with the living but psychic imprints that happen especially during moments of high tension, such as a murder or during intense moments of a person's life. According to the hypothesis, residual hauntings are simply non-interactive playbacks, similar to a movie.

While Wadsworth's residual haunting is clearly a Patriot, there's a similar story involving a British redcoat in the bowels of the Boylston T station, the oldest rapid transport platform in the United States. According to ghost tour Haunted Boston, there are reports of "a British soldier, in full redcoat regalia, standing in the middle of the tracks and holding a musket."

Trolley conductors usually see this gun-toting apparition during the early morning shift or the wee hours of the night. The ghostly trek from Arlington to Boylston is rumored to be a hazing ritual of sorts for new recruits. They slam on their brakes, obviously freaked out by the human-shaped mist, while the more experienced drivers get a kick out of spooking the newcomers.

Why would a Revolution-era casualty of war haunt Boylston station? During the gruesome excavation project in 1895, historian Samuel A. Green was called in to identify the skeletal remains of what turned out to be a mass grave site. "It is impossible to tell who is buried there, but we know the British during their eight months' occupancy of Boston in the revolutionary struggle, buried some of their soldiers who were killed at Bunker Hill there," he told the *Boston Daily Globe* in April 1895. "Others who died from the effects of wounds in this battle were also interred there."

The *Globe* reported that on the days the excavation took place, hordes of curious onlookers gathered around the dig site, prompting police to set up a barricade. A canvas had to be "spread over a couple of pieces of joint to shut off the view of the spectators in the vicinity of the tombs." Articles of hair and clothing were oddly well preserved within the subterranean pool of bodies, even though the battle occurred more than one hundred years before the dig. Some say many of the British soldiers were missing limbs and other body parts because of shoddy, pre-sterilization medical care. There's a generic gravestone at the Central Burying Ground honoring the desecrated 900 to 1,100 bodies uncovered during the trolley station excavation. The marker reads: "Here were re-interred the remains of persons found under the Boylston Street mall during the digging of the subway 1895."

Based on ghost lore, hauntings have been associated with the lack of proper burial or a later desecration of the grave. Countless spirits, according to paranormal researchers, have been traced to missing gravestones or vandalism of a resting place. In regard to the pre-Revolution spirit lingering in Wadsworth House, it's likely the residual haunting is a psychic imprint of sorts associated with the intense military strategy sessions in the summer of 1775.

In November 1973, the senior editor of *Harvard Magazine*, with offices formerly located in the Wadsworth House, wrote an article called "The House Is Haunted and We Like It That Way," referring to the tricorn hat wearing spirits said to haunt the almost three-hundred-year-old landmark. "For a society of rationalists, Harvardians are surprisingly interested in the supernatural," joked *Harvard Magazine*'s editor in 1998. "Clearly, all this talk about ghosts concerns Harvard's continuity and history and traditions—not séances and the ectoplasm."

Seriously? Based on reports from the cleaning lady who spotted the "grim character in a tricorn hat and cloak" levitating down the stairs, perhaps the ghosts of Harvard are more than a personification of the Ivy League's storied past. It's possible the spirits of Wadsworth House are, in fact, ghostly reminders of the historically significant military sessions spearheaded by the first president in 1775.

While the haunting at Wadsworth House is likely residual in nature, some believe Harvard's school spirit is actually a manifestation of Washington himself.

If the Revolutionary War–era ghost is the first president of the United States, why would he stick around Harvard's campus? Unlike his contemporaries including John Adams and Thomas Jefferson, Washington never attended college. He went to war instead. Washington's lack of a higher education seemed to be a point of contention for the leader throughout his illustrious career. It haunted him most of his life. Perhaps he's making a postmortem attempt at an Ivy League education.

JAMES MONROE

The last president from the George Washington–led Virginia dynasty, James Monroe served during the American Revolution and ultimately became president of the United States from 1817 to 1825. As an ambassador to France, he helped negotiate the Louisiana Purchase, resulting in the United States nearly doubling in size. As president, he signed the Missouri Compromise, which banned slavery in the northern territories.

His eight-year stint as the country's commander-in-chief, however, ended on a sour note.

He spent his final years in financial ruins and moved to New York City to live with his youngest daughter, Maria. She married into the wealthy Gouverneurs family and Monroe was buried in their vault at Manhattan's Marble Cemetery when he passed on July 4, 1831.

Michelle Hamilton, a Virginia-based author and former tour guide at the James Monroe Museum and Memorial Library, told me the founding father "is an underrated president, often overlooked compared to Jefferson and Madison," she said. "Monroe was an extremely popular president and his time in office was known as the 'Era of Good Feelings' because partisan politics were at an all-time low. It's something that has never been replicated."

Hamilton said Monroe and his daughters rebuilt the White House following the War of 1812 and many of the gilded beechwood pieces his family purchased during his presidency are still on display at 1600 Pennsylvania Avenue in Washington, D.C.

When I mentioned that Monroe's spirit has reportedly moved with his skeletal remains starting with Manhattan's Marble Cemetery where he was initially buried and then reappeared at Virginia's Hollywood Cemetery where he was reinterred, Hamilton was shocked. "I really can't think of a reason why he has been seen near his remains in Hollywood Cemetery," she said. "He died in New York and it was only several years later that he was moved to Richmond on the eve of the Civil War."

While Monroe supposedly keeps watch near his tomb in Richmond, the ghosts of his wife and daughters have been spotted at the White House and the nearby Stephen Decatur House in Lafayette Square. Monroe's wife, Elizabeth, was ill throughout most of his presidency and the duties of official White House hostess were assumed by their eldest daughter, Eliza Monroe Hay.

"Eliza earned a reputation as a bossy, self-centered, and somewhat vindictive hostess during the eight years she functioned as her father's official White House social director," wrote Charles Stansfield in *Haunted Presidents*. "Eliza's ghost is said to have shown up during James Buchanan's term, abrasively ordering servants about as they prepared the East Room for an important reception. Allegedly, the phantom was rude and disruptive, attempting to rearrange the place cards on the table. The ghost evaporated like fog in sunlight when the head butler showed up to see what the fuss was about."

The spirit of Monroe's youngest daughter, Maria, has been seen at the Stephen Decatur House where she held her wedding reception with her husband, Samuel Gouverneur. The home's owner, Decatur, was fatally wounded in a duel and was dropped off during the post-wedding bash. The celebration was ruined and the man of the house died in great pain. Maria's spirit reportedly appeared once on the anniversary of Decatur's death on March 20, 1920.

Hamilton said Monroe's daughters had strong personalities and it makes sense that they're lingering from beyond the grave. "He was a devoted family man and loved his wife and daughters deeply," Hamilton told me. "The Monroes were very private. He would write letters to his wife in French so they could converse in privacy."

When I asked Hamilton about Monroe's service during the American Revolution, she said he suffered from the bullet wound he received during the Battle of Trenton. "Shortly after the Virginians arrived, George Washington led the army in a retreat from New York City into New Jersey and then across the Delaware River into Pennsylvania," Hamilton said. "In December, Monroe took part in a surprise attack on a Hessian encampment. Though the attack was successful, Monroe suffered a severed artery in the battle and nearly died."

Hamilton told me Washington cited Monroe for his bravery and promoted him to captain. "After his wounds healed, Monroe returned to Virginia to recruit his own company of soldiers," she said.

When it comes to the ghosts of our country's dead presidents, Hamilton said it makes more sense for Monroe to visit his former home called Highland, formerly called Ash-Lawn Highland, near Thomas Jefferson's Monticello in Charlottesville, Virginia. "These were the men who helped create this country. I don't think he had any regrets," Hamilton said. "I wouldn't be surprised if they come in and check out what we are up to and how we are treating the country they left us."

Monroe and his family spent twenty-four years at Highland. Because of his growing personal debt, he was forced to sell the plantation house in 1825. Hamilton said it would make sense for the former president's spirit to revisit the Virginia house he shared with his beloved wife and daughters. "Monroe and the other founders were forced to be away from the homes and families they loved for years at a time," Hamilton said. "I always think they come back from time to time to just enjoy their homes again."

MONROE'S HAUNT: HOLLYWOOD CEMETERY

RICHMOND, VA—Why would the ghost of the fifth president of the United States guard his tomb nicknamed "The Birdcage" at Hollywood Cemetery in Richmond, Virginia? Perhaps his spirit was unnerved when his skeletal remains were disinterred from his original burial ground at Marble Cemetery in New York City's East Village.

James Monroe's ghost may have had a bone to pick when the governor of Virginia repatriated the dead president's remains in 1856, twenty-five years after his death in New York City. Based on the reports associated with Monroe's spirit, however, he hasn't been able to rest in peace for decades.

According to Charles Stansfield's *Haunted Presidents*, Monroe's spirit was confused when his corpse was moved from New York City to Richmond. "His ghost, it is said, hung around the Marble Cemetery in Lower Manhattan for a while, until it, too, migrated to Richmond."

Stansfield penned that the former president's ghostly manifestation, much like he appeared during his lifetime, was an imposing figure standing six feet tall with a muscular build. "Intelligence seems to shine from his eyes as the phantom surveys his surroundings," Stansfield wrote. "At first, it seems as though the spirit is trapped inside an elaborate cage, a gothic scrollwork of iron. But the wispy ghost passes through the ironwork as though it were not there—ghosts are not restricted by material barriers."

The author of *Haunted Presidents* commented that Monroe's spirit is "quietly reflective" adding that some report seeing the phantom rub his left shoulder, indicating pain associated with a bullet wound he received during the American Revolution. "Major James Monroe fought under General George Washington at the Battle of Trenton," Stansfield wrote. "In Emanuel Leutze's famous painting *Washington Crossing the Delaware*, Monroe is the one holding the flag. It took him three months to recover, and he carried the British bullet in him for the rest of his life."

When I asked Roxie Zwicker, author of *Massachusetts Book of the Dead*, if she thought moving Monroe's skeletal remains could result in his postmortem discontent, she said it's a possibility. Her personal experiences researching cemeteries, on the hand, suggested otherwise. "When I went to visit John and Abigail Adams's graves under the church in Quincy, I felt they were much happier having been moved from the cemetery across the street," Zwicker told me. "My belief is that in some cases yes, they might feel forgotten or not easily found. I also believe that some just want to rest their bones."

Bill Pavao, a historian based in Fall River, Massachusetts, told me Abigail Adams's spirit was initially out of sorts when she was moved from the Hancock Cemetery in Quincy to a chamber in the basement of the United First Parish Church. "Apparently, people used to see Abigail Adams's spirit crossing the street from the cemetery," Pavao told me. "There used to be a store called 'Abigail's Crossing' back in the day."

Pavao also cited a famous haunting associated with General Anthony Wayne. Remembered as "Mad Anthony" for his aggressive fighting style, Wayne stormed the British in Stony Point, New York, during the War of Independence and won the battle with a bloody, bayonets-only attack. He was initially buried in Eerie, Pennsylvania, in 1796. His family, however, wanted to move the Revolutionary War hero's remains closer to home in Radnor.

When the crew exhumed Wayne's corpse, they found it was in oddly good condition. So the excavators decided to scrape and boil away the flesh and then reinterred his remaining bones in Radnor. Pavao said Wayne's spirit was unhappy with the move. "He's buried in two places," Pavao told me. "Bones in one place, and his 'meat' in the other."

Also, Wayne's ghost apparently has a calendar.

According to legend, not all of his bones made it across the state, which made him even more "mad" in the afterlife. Wayne's spirit supposedly reanimates on his birthday, January 1, making the trek from Eerie to Radnor on U.S. Route 322 in Pennsylvania. His ghost reportedly follows the path where his bones were lost and he's desperately trying to recover them.

Why are skeletal remains so important to former luminaries like Wayne and Monroe? Peter Muise, author of *Witches and Warlocks of Massachusetts*, said they're spiritually significant. "In some cultures, bones are symbolic of the soul," Muise told me. "Unlike other parts of the body, they endure after death and so are considered eternal."

Based on Monroe's temperament in life, he's probably less emotional than Wayne about the cemetery switcheroo. "His ghost, reportedly, is calm and undramatic—so was the man," wrote Stansfield in *Haunted Presidents*.

Monroe stoically watches over his birdcage-style tomb at Hollywood Cemetery, making sure his decayed corpse survived the move from Manhattan to Virginia. And, no, he doesn't have a bone of contention. He's just guarding his skeletal remains as he massages his wounded left shoulder in a perpetual ghost loop.

JOHN ADAMS

Two-faced president? Not exactly. Based on reports and his well-kept journals, there were two sides to John Adams. Apparently, there were dueling aspects to the second president's personality that seemed to present itself over time.

During his youth, Adams was an optimistic leader. The Harvard educated firebrand became a vocal opponent of the Stamp Act of 1765, which required the colonies to pay a tax to England for stamped documents. He also supported the Boston Tea Party, a historic demonstration against the British's tea monopoly over colonial merchants, which unfolded on December 16, 1773.

Adams chronicled the fight for independence in his diaries and letters to his wife, Abigail, and colleague Thomas Jefferson. He also helped craft the Declaration of Independence and later served two terms as vice president under George Washington, but only one as president.

It was during this period that the second side of Adams's personality emerged. He became a beleaguered bureaucrat. During his four-year stint as president, the founding father signed the controversial Alien and Sedition Acts and lost the bid for a second term. His former friend Jefferson accused the commander-in-chief of despotism or trying to rule the country with absolute power.

Adams and his wife retired to their home in Quincy, Massachusetts, known as the Old House at Peacefield, which he acquired in 1787 after the property's Loyalist owners fled Massachusetts during the American Revolution. Adams eventually made amends with his friend Jefferson before he died on July 4, 1826. The second president was ninety years old.

The ghost of John Adams reportedly still lingers at Peacefield. There are, however, two versions of his spirit that reflect the youthful optimism that effectively ignited the Revolutionary War against Great Britain and the bitter man he became after losing the election for a second term as president of the United States.

Yes, his spirit has two faces.

His ghost has been spotted in the parlor of his home near Boston and seated on the low stone fence outside of Peacefield, according to Charles Stansfield's *Haunted Presidents*. "In the parlor manifestation, Adams's spirit appears in the form of advanced old age," wrote Stansfield. "He sits in an armchair reading, perhaps reminiscing about his long life of service to his country. His expression has been described as rather sad and lost in thought."

Stansfield reported that the second version of Adams's apparition seen perched outside of Peacefield was less resentful. "In contrast to the sour 'parlor ghost,' Adams's alternate manifestation, sitting on the stone fence outside his house, seems serenely content," Stansfield wrote. "This phantom appears to be looking over what were crop fields and pastures with satisfied contentment. Adams genuinely loved his home even though his duties had him living hundreds, even thousands, of miles away. He was intensely interested in scientific agriculture for the good reason that he needed to coax the maximum income from each acre."

Why two manifestations? I reached out to my friends in the paranormal community for answers and they told me it was a common occurrence, especially when it involves a person with such a significant historical legacy. "This is purely speculation, but perhaps those two ages during his lifetime were when he had his most profound memories at the actual location he haunts and he chooses to revisit that timeframe in his memory bank," said Rob Hernandez, host of the radio show *Live Paranormal*. "We've seen the same thing with Abraham Lincoln. His apparition has been spotted at his former home in Springfield, Illinois, and at the White House. Based on my experience, I would have to say both Adams and Lincoln are psychic imprints and not intelligent spirits."

Joni Mayhan, an author and empath, agreed with Hernandez. "Is it possible for one ghost to haunt multiple locations at the same time, presenting himself in vastly different roles? When it comes to the paranormal world, anything is conceivable," Mayhan told me. "When my friend Sandy and I were beginning to explore our mediumship abilities, we would often go into a haunted location armed with pen and paper. As soon as we felt a ghost drift in, we would write down what we felt and saw in our mind's eye and then share it once we were finished. We often saw the same person, but frequently perceived them at different ages. I always saw them younger than she did. Why is this?"

Mayhan said a spirit often presents itself to the living in a way it would like to be seen. "Sandy is ten years older than me, so it makes perfect sense for him to show himself to her as a peer of her similar age range. But what about a ghost who shows himself the same way to everyone in one location, but presents himself in a vastly different role in another location? In this case, I would say one or both instances are residual energy imprints. The man's connection to the land was so strong during his life, he left his mark."

As far as the two apparitions of Adams at his former home in Quincy, Mayhan believes they're both playback spirits. "When I think of residual energy, I always think about Gettysburg. Because of the brutal battle that occurred there, people frequently see soldiers marching across the fields," Mayhan said. "It's almost as though the energy surrounding the area recorded that moment, playing it back over and over for all eternity so no one could ever forget. I believe the same instance could have occurred with John Adams."

According to Mayhan, a face-to-face encounter with the ghostly duo doesn't necessarily mean double trouble. Instead, it's like a videotaped replay of events from two centuries ago.

In other words, the two manifestations of the founding father's spirit at Peacefield aren't ghosts in the traditional sense, but a benign residual haunting or a playback of past events that has psychically imprinted itself at the former president's home.

ADAMS'S HAUNT: MASSACHUSETTS HALL

CAMBRIDGE, MA—One restless spirit has taken the whole "pahk the cah in Hahvad Yahd" idiom quite literally . . . for almost a century. Massachusetts Hall has been Harvard's crown jewel, touted as the oldest building on the Cambridge campus and boasting a historical lineage that dates back to the country's second president, John Adams.

For the record, he shared a triple room on the first floor in the 1750s. Its solid brick façade has been a symbol of American intelligentsia and has been the Yard's tacit sentinel for almost three centuries, dating back to 1720.

The Early Georgian–style dorm and office building, which currently houses freshmen on the top floor and served as a temporary barracks for 640 Continental soldiers during the Siege of Boston during the Revolutionary War, is also notoriously haunted. "Eighteenth-century buildings should have ghosts," mused William C. "Burriss" Young, who lived in Mass Hall for decades as an assistant dean of freshmen. "If there are going to be ghosts, it makes sense they should live in the nicest building in the Yard."

According to campus lore, the resident ghost known as Holbrook Smith was a "tall respectable-looking older gentleman" who would chat up freshmen and claim to be among the class of 1914. The strange gentleman was most active around the B entryway of Massachusetts Hall, where he often spooked students.

"He was in his late fifties or early sixties—this was back in 1967–1968—and he was dressed in wing-tipped shoes and a tweed jacket, very Ivy," described E. Fred Yalouris to the *Crimson*. "The man came into the B entryway one day and knocked on our door. He proceeded to sit and talk, always 'very gracious and well-spoken.'" Young said Holbrook Smith "insisted he had lived in B entry and he had been roommates with Senator Saltonstall in the Class of 1914, but Senator Saltonstall had not lived in B entry."

Yalouris said Smith was "obviously an eccentric old gent" and he had the ability to "appear and disappear." The full-bodied apparition could travel through the building's brick façade. "One time he disappeared between the fourth and the first floor of the dorm," Yalouris said. "It was quite mysterious."

Smith returned to the dorm every fall for almost a century until Young confronted the so-called phantom and asked him to leave. He looked at the dean of freshmen with "the saddest eyes I've ever seen," recalled Young in an interview with *Harvard Magazine*, and said, "You've ruined a perfectly good thing."

Students and faculty have talked about hauntings at Harvard University's Massachusetts Hall for years. Thomas E. Crooks, a former administrator who passed away in 1998, told the *Harvard Crimson* in 1989 that "in Massachusetts Hall, there are a couple of ghosts who are passing as people." Crooks said he had close encounters with spirits roaming the halls of Harvard. "Every time I see one, I forget it right away," Crooks said. "It's such a traumatic experience that I erase it from my mind at once."

Although Smith hasn't been seen roaming Mass Hall since that mythic confrontation, tour guides with my former Cambridge Haunts ghost tour told me Smith's residual energy still lurks around the building. "He's made impromptu appearances on the tour and didn't like it when we talked about the way he looks," said tour guide Ashley Shakespeare, adding that he's a bit "uppity and protective" compared to other spirits on campus.

Several people who have taken photos of the building's exterior have captured odd orange light anomalies when Shakespeare alludes to Mass Hall's eccentric phantom. According to paranormal researchers, orange is a sign an entity has assumed the role of a protector or caretaker. So, Smith may be serving as the building's other-worldly sentry.

In the late 1970s, a noted clairvoyant visited the Massachusetts Hall dorm to investigate if residual spirits were indeed haunting Harvard's oldest building. "Students had expressed an interest in that sort of thing, and this lady had worked with the FBI in locating missing persons," Young recalled. "The speaker warned students that any photographs taken of her would not come out because of the strong supernatural presence in the room," reported the *Crimson*. "Sure enough, the photographs came out blank."

Around the corner from John Adams's old dormitory is Holden Chapel. Used as the first cadaver room when the college hosted the Harvard Medical College, the old structure is rumored to be teeming with ghosts from its past.

Built in 1744, the colonial-style building was the spiritual gathering place as well as a secular lecture hall for Harvard students until 1772. The chapel housed 160 soldiers from 1775 to 1776 in the days leading up to the American Revolution. It later became the hub of Harvard's burgeoning medical school, established in 1783 by John Warren, and served as a morgue for students in training for half a century.

One legend alludes to Holden Chapel's macabre medical history. According to the late William C. "Burriss" Young, who lived in nearby Mass Hall as an assistant dean of freshmen, there's a female spirit that returns to Holden Chapel every year "around the first snowstorm." Her name? Pickham.

According to Young, she was "a woman who was riding with her fiancé in a sleigh through the square when their horse slipped on the ice and their sleigh flipped over. Her fiancé broke his neck and died in her arms." According to the legend, he was buried at the Old Burying Ground, but "when she returned to visit the grave, the body had been dug up and stolen."

Back in the day, resurrection men—or grave robbers—would keep careful track of who died and where they were buried. When there was an opportunity to sell a body to a medical school, the resurrection man would go and dig up someone recently deceased. It was common practice for people like Ephraim Littlefield, who was a janitor at the Harvard Medical School and rumored to be a grave robber, to retrieve a dead body when the medical school's stock of cadavers was getting low.

The female spirit allegedly haunting Holden Chapel "became convinced her husband's body was in Holden Chapel, which housed the dissecting labs at that time," continued Young. "Every year, at the first snowstorm, she would escape from her family's house in New Bedford and try to break into Holden Chapel and would have to be physically restrained from entering. She's still spotted from time to time," Young told the *Crimson* in 1997. "And if you ever see her, and you observe carefully, you'll notice she doesn't leave any footprints in the snow."

With such a macabre legacy, Holden Chapel today looks like a throwback to Harvard's days of yore. For most of the twentieth century, it hosted the Harvard Glee Club and later the Radcliffe Choral Society. The chapel was renovated in 1999, and archaeologists discovered human remains in the building's basement. "My first thought was, 'Oooohh, an old Harvard murder,'" said Associate Professor of Anthropology

Carole A.S. Mandryk in a *Harvard Crimson* interview published in 1999. "They're definitely human bones."

According to the report, workers found several sawed-open skeletons, broken scientific glassware, and test tubes strewn among the remains. "Between 1782 and 1850, part of the basement was used as an anatomy and dissection lecture hall for the Medical School," wrote the *Crimson*. "Some of the bones have metal pieces sticking out of them, as if someone was trying to construct a skeleton," Mandryk added.

Remember the wailing female spirit known as Pickham that returns to Holden Chapel during the first snowstorm? She hasn't been spotted since the building's renovations. It's possible she was right and her husband's remains were buried in the basement. Perhaps Pickham finally got some closure beyond the grave when the bones were unearthed and removed from Holden Chapel.

PAUL REVERE

What really happened at Old North Church on April 18, 1775? The famous "one if by land, two if by sea" line from Henry Wadsworth Longfellow's poem *Paul Revere's Ride* is based on actual events orchestrated by Revere and carried out by Old North Church's sexton, or the church's caretaker, Robert Newman. Revere's friend and the church's vestryman, Captain John Pulling Jr., was also there to warn the Sons of Liberty that General Thomas Gage and his British troops were coming.

Two lanterns, held that fateful night at the top of Old North Church's wooden steeple, ignited what would become the beginning of the American Revolution.

"Revere enlisted the help of over thirty additional riders. He placed them across the river in Charlestown and ordered the militia leaders to look to the steeple of Old North Church every night for signal lanterns, the number of which indicated when the British army was leaving Boston and by which route," the Old North Foundation explained on their website. "One lit lantern meant the British would march over the Boston Neck, a narrow strip of land and the only road connecting the town to the mainland, which would take a considerable amount of time. Two lit lanterns in the steeple meant the British would take a shortcut by rowing boats across the Charles River into Cambridge, cutting valuable time off their journey."

Newman climbed up the staircases in the back corners of Old North Church and scurried up eight flights of stairs in complete darkness. He lit two lanterns with flint and steel at the top of the steeple and held them for about one minute toward Charlestown, alerting Revere's men, which included the often-overlooked William Dawes.

General Gage, who coincidentally worshipped at Old North Church, was greeted by an armed militia in Lexington. And the rest, as they say, was history.

With such an important role in the days leading up to the American Revolution, it should come as no surprise that one of the nation's most historic churches also brims with the spirits of those who lived and died there during its hundreds of years of tumultuous history. The late Jim McCabe, a noted ghost lore expert, believed the historic Revolutionary War–era buildings such as Old North Church are ghost magnets. "The old Yankees may have been strange in some ways, but they kept the old buildings, which has made it attractive to many visitors—even ghosts," McCabe told the *Boston Globe*. "Spirits are attracted to places they lived in. I think what attracts ghosts up here is that you don't tear down the buildings."

Built in 1723 by William Prince, Old North is the oldest standing church building in Boston. The famous steeple, which can be seen at various spots throughout Boston and the harbor, fell during Hurricane Carol in 1854. It was fully restored the following year. For the record, it was also blown down by the great gale in 1804 and rebuilt in 1807. And yes, Old North is believed to be haunted.

According to Pam Bennett, retail manager at the popular tourist attraction, the building's former sexton had a close encounter with the misty outlines of three Revolutionary War–era men. "He said they were as clear as day," Bennett told me, adding that the church's sexton was a skeptic and was a bit shocked to run into three full-bodied apparitions at the Salem Street church. "He told them he's just doing his job and he noticed their eyes followed him. When he returned, they were gone."

Bennett also mentioned that a woman, who lived in the brownstone next to Old North, banged on the gift-shop door one day and claimed a boy buried beneath the church regularly visited her North End home. "We told her we do have unmarked graves beneath the church."

In fact, thirty-seven crypts, buried beneath the structure, contain the remains of over one thousand former members of Old North Church. But why would a nineteenth-century boy haunt the church's North End neighbor?

Salem Street Academy, a schoolhouse on the north side of the church property, was built in 1810. Boston's first Sunday school got its start at the academy, opening its doors to the city's children in 1815. Co-owned by the church, the Sunday school became popular and welcomed thousands of students, recalled Dr. Charles Downer in his account published in 1893. Henry Ward Beecher, a famous Civil War–era abolitionist, was one of the school's alumni. Beecher's sister, Harriet, penned the anti-slavery manifesto *Uncle Tom's Cabin*. The school was replaced by the parish house in 1848 and was officially closed in 1908.

Believe it or not, the woman who had a face-to-face encounter with the ghost boy wearing period garb lives in the exact location that was formerly home to Salem Street Academy. While no reports of untimely deaths at the school in the 1800s can be found, it's common for spirits to return to a place they frequented. "A person doesn't have to die at a location for it to become haunted," wrote Joni Mayhan in *Dark and Scary Things*. "They return because it's a comfortable place for them."

And what about the three Revolutionary War–era spirits spotted by Old North Church's sexton? Mayhan said it's common for ghosts to frequent churches because of guilt over a past deed. "If they feel their sin is great enough, they might balk at crossing over into the light out of fear of where it will bring them," Mayhan continued. "By dwelling at a church, they might feel closer to God and hope to find redemption for their sins."

Of course, hundreds of former parishioners are buried in the labyrinthine crypts in the bowels of Old North Church. While spirits find solace in these places of worship, the emotions associated with important events—like a marriage or even a funeral—can also linger within these hallowed and often historic walls.

Is Revere haunting Old North Church or even his former colonial-era home in Boston's North End? Probably not. The famous minuteman's spirit is rumored to make the rounds near his grave marker at Granary Burial Ground on Tremont Street. In fact, some say his spirit sits upon the horse on which he made his famous midnight ride and he continues to guard the hallowed grounds of Boston's third oldest cemetery in the afterlife.

REVERE'S HAUNT: WARREN TAVERN

CHARLESTOWN, MA—The oldest tavern in Massachusetts and arguably America's most historic watering hole, Warren Tavern on

Pleasant Street was one of the first buildings constructed after the British set Charlestown ablaze in June 1775. Built in 1780, the tavern hosted Revolutionary War luminaries like Paul Revere and Benjamin Franklin. Our nation's first president, George Washington, even stopped by in 1789 for some post-war reverie.

Based purely on its historic legacy, Warren Tavern should be haunted, right? MaryLee Trettenero, a Charlestown-based tour guide and author, strongly believes it is. "When we do paranormal investigations with equipment, we first ask the manager if anyone has seen apparitions," she told the *Boston Globe* in 2015. "One of the waitstaff has seen a Victorian woman dressed in black in the front room of the Warren Tavern. This is also where most of the paranormal activity registers on our devices when we do investigations."

Trettenero said the waitstaff has spotted a Revolutionary War–era man in a wig and tights from across the bar and near the porthole window. The bar manager said he has heard the sound of high-heels clicking outside of his office when no one is there.

In the past, she's even claimed to have been visited by the spirit of Daniel Webster while eating from the tavern's tasty pub-grub menu. She also features the haunted hotspot on her Spirits of Charlestown historic ghost tour. Dining with the dead? Yep, Warren Tavern is said to have a few spirits and not the kind poured from a bottle.

The tavern is named after Dr. Joseph Warren, an outspoken opponent of the British and a notorious hellraiser. Almost forgotten in history, it was Warren who directed the team of minutemen, including Paul Revere and William Dawes, to warn Samuel Adams that the regulars were coming. Elected as the second general in command of the Massachusetts forces on June 14, 1775, he was savagely killed three days later while leading troops at the Battle of Bunker Hill. He was killed instantly by a musket-ball shot to the head. Adding to the overkill, he was stripped of his clothing and savagely stabbed with a bayonet until he was unrecognizable. His lifeless body was dumped into a shallow ditch but his remains were identified ten months later thanks to a false tooth crafted by Revere.

Michael Baker, a paranormal investigator with Para-Boston, said he was wicked excited to check out the alleged activity at Warren's namesake tavern in 2011. "When we were asked to investigate this amazing place, our imaginations ran wild with the thoughts of all of the history-making discussions that must have been had by heroes and legends over a pint of frothy beer," he recalled. "The claims of activity at this place were what would be expected. Disembodied footsteps, apparitions of old patrons, and the uneasy feelings that go along with being in the cellar."

Baker said his team followed strict, science-based protocol when they investigated the tavern. "The first thought I had when entering this place was that there must be a ton of misinterpretations," he wrote in his investigation notes. "The floorboards creaked when the wind blew and the classic tavern design of the place certainly entertained the idea that some old drunkards must still be lingering in the corners. Shadows were plentiful here, but sadly, not the moving kind."

Members of the investigation team did feel some unusual heaviness in the basement, but that could be attributed to the low ceilings and wiring. "After setting up our equipment for the night, we all found a place to sit and hunkered down waiting for any signs of activity," he recalled. "The apparitions were said to appear at a certain table and were only visible in the mirror behind the bar. Unusual, but with that in mind we were careful to play by the guidelines. A set of eyes and a camera gazing endlessly into the mirror."

In a sit-down interview with *Ghosts of the American Revolution*, Baker and Para-Boston investigator Bart Smith said the ghosts said to haunt the watering hole were basically debunked. "We didn't encounter anything but we did debunk a few things," Baker said. "One of the claims is that the bar manager could hear the floorboards creaking. We determined the heat in the building moved the boards and it sounded like footsteps."

Smith said the team also found a legitimate explanation for the man-in-tights apparition often spotted at a table after the bar closed. "The way the mirror was set up, it was almost a perfect explanation because the reflection of a lamp could easily be misinterpreted. At the corner of your eye, it did look like a person."

Baker said his team spent hours checking out the mirror. "It did look like a flesh-colored reflection of a man in colonial garb, but it was an optical illusion caused by the lamp," he continued. "We did hear what sounded like a rattling-around noise in the kitchen that couldn't be explained," added Smith.

The Para-Boston investigators said the team talked with the bar manager and employees about the alleged activity and they were still convinced the watering hole was indeed haunted. Both Baker and Smith said Warren Tavern's history alone is enough to warrant further investigation.

"I was watching the *Sons of Liberty* show on TV and they were talking about a tavern. I assumed it was this tavern because they were talking about Joseph Warren," Smith continued. "There is so much history here it's hard to rule it out."

While Baker's team carried out a sound, scientific investigation and found little-to-no evidence, he's not completely shutting the door on the possibility. "We didn't have any experiences but it doesn't mean there isn't something here," Baker explained. "If we had to make a guess based on our investigation, we would have to say it's not haunted."

BOSTON'S SPIRITS OF '76

There definitely were tunnels underneath the North End.
—Peter Muise, *New England Folklore Blog*

Boston, Massachusetts, is a hotbed of paranormal activity. Whether you're a believer or not, there are more than a few skeletons in the city's collective closet. Many of those four-hundred-year-old secrets can be found in the buildings and landmarks scattered throughout the historic city. In fact, many of the spirits allegedly lingering in Boston might be a byproduct of the strong-willed New England desire to maintain the old buildings of the past, which act as lures to both visitors and ghosts.

"Spirits are attracted to the places they lived in," opined the late Jim McCabe, who was a noted ghost lore expert in Boston. "I think what attracts ghosts up here is that you don't tear down the buildings."

Adam Berry, co-star of *Kindred Spirits* and paranormal investigator formerly from *Ghost Hunters,* echoed McCabe's theory. "Because of the history, there are so many interesting places that could be investigated. It was one of the biggest seaports in the country and had tons of activity during the Revolutionary and Civil Wars. There must be spirits left behind, mulling about and checking out the status of the community they built way back when."

During his four-year collegiate stint in Boston, Berry said he fell in love with the Hub. "Boston's rich history and the singular fact that it was the cornerstone of the American Revolution makes it a city that is truly one of a kind," Berry said. "Why would anyone want to leave . . . even after they're dead?"

Some skeletons emerged when visitors least expected it. In January 2009, a tourist fell into an unmarked crypt at the Granary Burial Ground during a self-guided tour and got up close and personal with one of the cemetery's tombs, which measures eight by twelve feet in size and is believed to be the grave of an eighteenth-century selectman, Jonathan Armitage. The visitor wasn't hurt, nor did he fall into the actual crypt; instead, it was the stairway leading to the vault.

In 2007, a mysterious sinkhole emerged at King's Chapel Burying Ground, a historic cemetery dating back to 1757 near

Government Center and across from the haunted Omni Parker House. "Beneath the crumbling earth are stairs leading down to the family crypt," reported the *Boston Herald* in January 2007. "It's unclear why this grave in particular is giving way, though time and weather are chief among the suspected causes." The sinkhole, which was blocked off from pedestrians with a black steel cage, continued to baffle the burial ground's conservators for years.

King's Chapel Burying Ground was the scene of several historical tales from the crypt, including reports of a man who was rumored to be buried alive in 1820. One elderly woman strongly believed that a nineteenth-century property owner was buried six feet under by his family in an attempt to get possession of his wealth. An angry mob gathered around the burial ground, demanding authorities exhume the body. Doctors investigated, and it was announced he was dead as a doornail. However, the woman continued to believe that the death occurred as the result of him being buried alive.

In 1775, the lauded editor of the *Columbian Centinel,* Benjamin Russell, had an encounter with the supernatural when the historic cemetery on the corner of Tremont and School Streets was known as Stone Chapel. "It was part of my duty as an assistant in the domestic affairs of the family to have the care of the cow. One evening, after it was quite dark, I was driving the cow to her pasturage—the Common. Passing by the burial-ground, adjoining the Stone Chapel, I saw several lights that appeared to be springing from the earth, among the graves, and immediately sinking again to the ground. To my young imagination, they could be nothing but ghosts," Russell recounted in *The Pilgrims of Boston* by Thomas Bridgman.

Russell continued: "I left the cow to find her way to the Common and ran home at my utmost speed. Having told my father the cause of my fright, he took me to the spot where the supposed ghosts were still leaping and playing their pranks. When, lo! There was the sexton, throwing out as he was digging fragments of decayed coffins. The phosphorus in the decayed wood blending with the peculiar state of the atmosphere, presented the appearance that had completely unstrung my nerves, and terrified me beyond description. I was never afterwards troubled with the fear of ghosts."

While most paranormal experts cite Boston Common's Central Burying Ground as the most haunted cemetery in Boston, the older

King's Chapel Burying Ground—built in 1630 and hosting a slew of Puritan founders, including Governor John Winthrop, Reverend John Cotton, and Mary Chilton (the first woman to walk off the *Mayflower*)—boasts a few ghostly legends of its own. Included in these is the strange story of roaming spirits looking for their markers. In 1810, there was a switcheroo of sorts when the superintendent of burials moved most of the headstones at the cemetery and laid them out in neat rows closer to the center of the yard. The legend states that the moving of the headstones confused the spirits so much that ever since they've wandered aimlessly looking for their graves.

Incidentally, the cemetery is built adjacent to King's Chapel, an Anglican church. Many of the big-name burials were Puritan elders who left England in search of religious freedom. Ironically, their final resting place is next to the church from which they fled.

In addition to the wandering-ghost myth, a macabre story associated with the churchyard states that a woman is buried there whose head was cut off and placed between her legs. The story goes that the carpenter built the woman's coffin too small and, in an attempt to cover his blunder, decapitated the corpse, placed the head inside the coffin, and nailed the lid shut. No proof exists as to the legend's truth.

Not far from King's Chapel is Boston's North End. Based purely on aesthetics, Paul Revere's old neighborhood should be haunted. In fact, horror writer H.P. Lovecraft believed the North End was fertile ground for the supernatural. In *Pickman's Model,* the author convincingly wrote about the inexplicable magic of the North End's spirited underbelly, adding that "the whole North End once had a set of tunnels that kept certain people in touch with each other's houses, and the burying ground and the sea." He also talked about the lack of ghosts in Boston's Back Bay saying the newly created land around Newbury Street hasn't been around long enough "to pick up memories and attract local spirits."

The Reverend Cotton Mather, along with his influential family members including his Harvard president father Increase, is buried in the Mather Tomb in the Copp's Hill Cemetery in the North End. "The second-oldest cemetery in Boston, Copp's Hill was established in 1659 and is filled with famous figures such as Cotton and Increase Mather, as well as former slaves and revolutionary soldiers," reported the website OnlyInYourState. "Some say the hallowed ground is haunted by the spirit of Increase Mather, a fierce and imposing colonial preacher who condemned many of the so-called Salem witches to hell."

While the blogger probably mixed up the Harvard president with his witch-hunting son, the legend associated with the lingering spirit at Copp's Hill suggests it's the Rev. Cotton Mather and not his dad, Increase. "Some visitors see glowing orbs of light appear amongst the tombstones, while others say they have felt unseen bodies brush against them in the dark," the website claimed.

Is Copp's Hill Cemetery haunted by Cotton? It's possible. However, locals in the North End notoriously remain tight-lipped about the neighborhood's ghost lore.

Michael Baker, former head of the group called the New England Center for the Advancement of Paranormal Science (NECAPS) and member of Para-Boston, leaves no gravestone unturned when he investigates a so-called haunted location, which includes a few of the old structures in the North End. Baker said he's heard very few reports of ghosts in the historic buildings surrounding Copp's Hill Cemetery. Why? He believes it's a cultural thing.

"The North End seems a bit devoid of claims," Baker said when asked about the lack of alleged paranormal activity in the historically Italian neighborhood. "I have always felt much of it has to do with the religious views of the people who live there. There are a lot of old-school Italian families there, people who tend to be well embedded in religious culture. I have noticed this old-world approach to religion often brings with it an unspoken rule about dabbling in or acknowledging things related to the paranormal."

Oddly, one of Boston's more infamous made-up ghost stories involves a man leaving his home from Middle Street in the North End. William Austin's literary character Peter Rugg—who stubbornly rode his horse into a thunderstorm in 1770 and was cursed to drive his carriage until the end of time—was completely fabricated. However, people over the years have reportedly spotted the ghostly man with his daughter by his side frantically trying to make the trek back to Boston.

According to the legend, Rugg was visiting Concord with his daughter and stopped by a tavern recommended to him by a longtime friend before heading back to Boston. A violent thunderstorm was heading in their direction and the watering hole's owner insisted that Rugg and his daughter stay the night. Rugg, a notoriously defiant old man, refused the offer and headed directly into the storm. The horse and its driver never returned to Boston. However, people claimed to have seen what was called the "Storm-breeder," a phantom carriage driven by Rugg and considered to be the precursor to a thunderstorm, all over New England. One man in Connecticut said he had a face-to-face encounter with the ghost. "I have lost the road to Boston. My name is Peter Rugg," the specter supposedly said before vanishing into thin air.

As far as hauntings associated with the North End, Baker said it's possible, but he's not entirely convinced. "There are some claims in the North End," he said. "I know there are stories about the tunnels there. I have had a few calls from the North End over the years, but unfortunately they never amounted to anything significant."

Baker told me he hasn't found anything substantial while investigating there and finds the locals to be unusually tight-lipped. "I know several old Italian families and they won't even embrace a discussion about ghosts," he said. "To them it's religiously forbidden. Of course, this is just my speculation but it's a pattern I've seen in people I speak with."

While the North End is mysteriously devoid of reported ghost sightings, the legends associated with its series of rumored underground tunnels seem to be based on reported fact. "There definitely were tunnels underneath the North End," explained Peter Muise, author of *Witches and Warlocks of Massachusetts*. "For example, in the nineteenth century construction workers discovered that a house at 453 Commercial Street had an archway in its cellar that connected to a large tunnel. It led from Commercial Street up toward Salem Street. Unfortunately this house was demolished in 1906 and the tunnel entrance along with it."

Who built the tunnels? Muise said they were probably built in the 1700s by Thomas Gruchy, a privateer who became wealthy from raiding Spanish ships. "He invested his loot in several Boston businesses, including a distillery, a warehouse, and several wharves. His wealth was excessive even for a privateer, and many of his neighbors suspected he was somehow smuggling goods into Boston without having to pay the British tariffs. Despite his shady background he became a prominent member of Boston society. He purchased the Salem Street mansion of former Governor Phipps in 1745, threw lavish parties, and became a congregant at the Old

North Church. Four plaster angels he looted from a French ship still decorate the church today."

Gruchy mysteriously disappeared in the 1700s and left behind a legacy of underground tunnels and stolen goods. "At the height of his wealth and popularity Gruchy vanished from Boston and was never seen again," Muise explained. "It's believed he was smuggling goods past the British using a series of underground tunnels, and fled town when they discovered what he was doing. Sadly his mansion on Salem Street was torn down years ago."

Muise said many secrets are buried beneath the North End's bloodstained soil. "A few other North End tunnels have been found," he said. "A book from 1817 mentions a tunnel under a house on Lynn Street, and a guide to Boston architecture notes that the cellar of a house on Salem Street still has an entrance to a tunnel in its basement. It has been bricked off so it's not clear where the tunnel goes or what it was used for."

Perhaps the ghosts of the North End are hiding in these hidden tunnels? Yes, it's possible they're lurking in the shadows beneath the cobblestone streets traveled by thousands of tourists flocking to a neighborhood famous for its old-school Italian eateries, Paul Revere, and the Mather family's tomb.

TOWN CRIER Q&A: GEOFFREY CAMPBELL

It's quite eerie to sit on a hill at night and hear rattling metal and disembodied voices calling for water and their mothers.
—Geoffrey Campbell, Plymouth Night Tour

Geoffrey Campbell, owner and operator of the Plymouth Night Tour, wears many hats. In addition to leading ghost lore enthusiasts up and down the haunted streets of "America's Hometown," he's the commander of the End Zone Militia, a group of rabble-rouser reenactors responsible for holding down the fort during halftime at Gillette Stadium.

Campbell and his crew of musket-wielding minutemen get to play dress up at Patriots games and act out one of New England's more legendary blasts from the past. "It's definitely a weird moment when you suddenly realize you're experiencing something exactly as another person would have 250 years ago," Campbell told me. "It's like time travel."

During the off-season, Campbell dons his historically accurate gear and tricorn cap for special gatherings at historic Revolutionary War–era sites scattered throughout the East Coast. "Whether it's on a battlefield, in an encampment, lying on a blanket looking up

Photo courtesy Geoffrey Campbell

at the stars with no man-made lights, it's beautiful and amazing," he said. "If you add the paranormal and ghostly aspect on top of it, then it can be downright freaky."

In the interview, Campbell talked about Plymouth's spirits of '76 and weighed in on the concept that reenactors somehow stir the pot of paranormal activity. Is there a residual energy still lingering at the battlefields of the American War of Independence? Yes, he believes there's an "aura of disaster" embedded in the bloodstained soil and the "give me liberty or give me death" battle cries from the fallen soldiers can still be heard in the afterlife.

Q: Have you encountered Revolutionary War–era spirits while giving tours in Plymouth, Massachusetts?
A: Yes, definitely. There's the ghost of naval captain Jacob Taylor lingering at Old Burial Hill and I had a weird experience of sensing a ship at sea near the gravestone of Captain Simeon Sampson. There's no shortage of Revolutionary War spirits in Plymouth such as the sailors from the *General Arnold* including Captain James Magee.

Q: What sort of paranormal activity have you experienced in Concord, Massachusetts?
A: I've always been curious about some of the sites along Battle Road, especially Bloody Angle. I definitely would like to do an investigation there at some point to see if any of the eight British soldiers killed there continue to linger. However, my only experience there was at Concord's Colonial Inn. I had my covers pulled up one night when I was staying over.

Q: Do you feel a connection to the Patriot spirits from New England's past?
A: Definitely. Having veterans of the conflict in my family heritage on both sides, I've always felt a pull.

Q: Do you think Revolutionary War reenactors could somehow trigger residual hauntings?
A: Of course because we dress and try to act like people of that time. It makes total sense that a spirit of that time would be attracted to us or question who we really are. They also could mistake us for someone they knew.

Q: Cemeteries with ties to the American Revolution like Plymouth's Burial Hill seem to be hotbeds of paranormal activity. Why?
A: I believe cemeteries to be more of a visitation site for those on the other side. The greater the number of burials from that period the more likely the visitations.

Q: Based on your experience, why do spirits from the Revolutionary War still linger?
A: Sometimes I question whether these spirits realize they're dead now that the war is long over. It's possible they don't realize they've passed.

Q: Why would an object from hundreds of years ago still have spirit energy attached to it?
A: All things are made of energy in one form or another and energy can transfer from a person to an object. Does a cold cup get warm when you hold it? Yes. With that same idea, a musket or a sword could have energy attached to it. I can see anything being infused with a person's energy, especially a prized possession or a personal weapon.

Q: If you had to pinpoint a location with a high level of spirits associated with the American Revolution, where would it be and why do you think this spot is so active?
A: I know for a fact that the Saratoga Battlefield is quite active on the anniversary of the battle. I experienced that myself a number of years ago and was told about the hauntings by one of the park rangers at Minuteman Park in Concord who had been stationed there. It's quite eerie to sit on a hill at night and hear rattling metal and disembodied voices calling for water and their mothers.

THE
OVERLOOKED

Abigail Adams sent a letter to her husband on March 31, 1776, urging him to "remember the ladies."
Photo by Jason Baker

ABIGAIL ADAMS

Dressed in a cap and lace shawl, Abigail Adams has reportedly been seen with her arms outstretched as if she was carrying laundry to the East Room of 1600 Pennsylvania Avenue. Misogynistic? Yes.

The former first lady who spent one term at what was then the newly built White House deserves a better ghost story. Adams probably rolled over in her burial crypt next to her president husband and son at United First Parish Church in Quincy, Massachusetts, when she learned about the laundry-in-hand stereotype.

Truthfully, Adams played a pivotal role in witnessing and recording the American Revolution from her South Shore home. She was also close friends with Mercy Otis Warren, a Plymouth-based author known for satirical essays that criticized the colonial government.

Adams and Warren met in 1773 and developed a life-long friendship. Warren's husband, James, and his brother Joseph were also major players during the War of Independence and they often hosted patriot leaders like John and Abigail and their cousin Sam Adams at their home in Plymouth.

The two women forged a powerful sisterhood even though they were sixteen years apart in age. They were both passionate about the need for independence from Great Britain and feverishly recorded the military conflicts unfolding around them including the Battle of Bunker Hill.

In 1776, Abigail sent a letter to Mercy complaining about her husband John after he laughed at her "remember the ladies" plea. Based on his response, Abigail felt subordinate to her husband and that he was unnecessarily patronizing to her.

While we're not sure if Mercy responded to Abigail's correspondence, we do know Warren left an equally indelible mark on local history. "Her town home and gravesite are on my regular tour route," said Vicki Noel Harrington, a guide and historian based in Plymouth, Massachusetts.

"Women's history is often overlooked but she was a published author, a member of a prominent family, and married to a general. It's tough to completely overlook Mercy."

Harrington said Warren's biggest contribution to the cause, like her friend Abigail, was her written word. "She published political essays and satirical plays before and during the Revolution," Harrington said. "She was also a well-respected and well-known member of the community. She would have been in a position to encourage other women to do simple things like participate in boycotts."

She and her husband, General James Warren, were opposed to some of the semantics contained within the Constitution, Harrington explained. "Some would argue that her 1788 pamphlet, *Observations on the New Constitution*, influenced the drafting of The Bill of Rights," Harrington told me. "It most definitely put her at odds with her dear friends John and Abigail Adams."

Harrington had a bizarre experience while giving a tour with the now-defunct Colonial Lantern Tours a few years ago. A woman came up to her after the ghost walk and repeated three times, "He kept telling me to ask you about Mercy." Harrington still isn't sure who "he" is but, after that ominous message, she started to include Warren's gravesite on her tour. "I would get a hit on my EMF meter when I shared her story and asked if any of the Warrens were present and pleased I was keeping her story alive," Harrington continued.

Mercy's friend Abigail was catapulted into the limelight when her husband became vice president for two terms and then president. In addition to her ghost supposedly haunting the White House, Adams has been spotted outside of her burial vault in Quincy and at a site called Penn's Hill near her family's South Shore homestead.

"A cairn, a pile of loose stones in a beehive shape, was erected in Abigail's memory atop Penn's Hill, from which vantage point Abigail had once observed the Battle of Bunker Hill," wrote Charles Stansfield in *Haunted Presidents*. "There, at her cairn, Abigail's disembodied spirit watches anxiously as American soldiers win a key, early battle. This manifestation would seem to be more characteristic of this very intelligent and public-spirited first lady than the simple domesticity of the laundry-hanger image."

Agreed. Both Adams and Warren deserve to be recognized for their contributions to the fight for independence. They weren't subservient housewives and were important based on their correspondence chronicling the war. If there is an actual residual haunting of a woman doing laundry in the White House, it's not how Abigail should be remembered by history.

ADAMS'S HAUNT: LONG ISLAND

BOSTON HARBOR, MA—If there's one Boston Harbor legend that could rival Georges Island's Lady in Black, it would be the Woman in Scarlet Robes. She's often overshadowed by the ghostly theatrics of the Southern belle believed to haunt Fort Warren, but Long Island's resident phantom had an equally traumatic demise.

In contrast to her made-up counterpart Melanie Lanier from the Confederacy, the lady in red seems to be historically viable. In other words, the Woman in Scarlet Robes may actually be based on fact. She's a true ghost of the American Revolution, an embodiment of the chaos that unfolded in Boston Harbor on March 17, 1776.

Her name was Mary Burton and she's sometimes still seen walking along Long Island's shoreline, covered in blood and looking for her husband. People claim to hear this wailing woman's specter begging for help.

On what the locals know as Evacuation Day and everyone else calls St. Patrick's Day, attempts by the British to siege Boston were foiled by George Washington, who occupied Dorchester Heights. According to the diary of the soon-to-become first lady Abigail Adams while living in Braintree, more than 170 British vessels were in Boston Harbor that day and only 78, including the infamous *Somerset*, fled. Almost 100 British vessels carrying thousands of redcoat soldiers and Tory refugees hovered around Long Island for weeks.

On June 13, 1776, American soldiers occupied Long Island and started bombing the British vessels to force them to leave.

According to Edward Rowe Snow, Burton's husband William was with his wife on one of the remaining British ships. "Mary had become friendly with three other women and on the day of the bombardment started and she was visiting their quarters," wrote Snow in *The Islands of Boston Harbor.* "The first cannonball that hit the ship passed through the open port and mortally wounded Mrs. Burton. Still conscious, Mary pleaded with her husband."

Ghost lore speculates the dying woman knew her wound was fatal and she begged her husband to bury her on the mainland. "I know I'm to die, William, but please don't let them bury me in the sea," she supposedly said. "William, bury me ashore."

William covered his wife in a red blanket and delicately lifted her into a small boat. He paddled to Long Island and begged the Americans to let him ashore. Her last words to him, according to legend, were "promise you'll come back for me. Promise me, William."

She wanted a proper burial at King's Chapel. He swore he would someday return, tears streaming down his face. Burton carried his dead wife onto the shore of Long Island near the present-day home of the lighthouse.

"A brief service was held, after which Mary Burton was buried," wrote Snow. The American soldiers on the island swore they would put her name on a gravestone and the Tory sympathizer left his wife in a makeshift grave. He returned to the British vessel and quickly headed back to his homeland.

Burton never returned to Long Island to give his wife a proper burial. According to Snow, he died near the turn of the century and the Americans on Long Island crafted a wooden headstone to mark Mary's remains. The marker slowly started to rot from the elements and from years of neglect.

It's said the ghost of Mary Burton, wearing a red cloak, walks the shores of Long Island waiting for her husband to return. In 1804 a group of fishermen claimed to have heard moans followed by a face-to-face encounter with the lady in red. "They saw the form of a woman wearing a scarlet cloak coming over the hill," Snow continued. "It appeared as though blood was streaming down her cloak from a terrible wound to her head, but she kept on walking, soon disappearing over the hill."

The encounters continued for years after the American Revolution and even the Civil War. "Soldiers stationed at Fort Strong reported other ghostly sightings while on patrol," wrote Christopher Forest in *Boston's*

Haunted History. "Rumors started to spread about the ghostly vision of a woman dressed in scarlet visiting the fort. Following the war, the rumors subsided until the 1890s, when a man named William Liddell, a private on the island, spotted the same lady. She came toward him with a distinct moan forming on her lips. Eventually, she disappeared into the chilly Atlantic air."

Mary Burton's tragic death, which is unverified, is just one of many tragedies that has left its indelible imprint on Long Island's blood-stained soil. During the colonial era, Native Americans lived on the longest island in Boston Harbor. At one mile and three-quarters, its land was fertile and full of natural resources. It became a farming community during the 1640s and then a Native American dumping ground during the 1670s.

Hundreds of natives were loaded on barges and transported to Deer Island. One colony of natives were sent to Long Island, which proved to be a resource-rich alternative to what Native Americans called Devil's Island, or Deer Island, located across Boston Harbor. At least, on Long Island, the decimated natives could harvest clams and fish.

During the 1800s, the island was being groomed to be a summer resort. The Long Island Company built several inns, including one in the center, which was described as "a splendid hotel, large and accommodating, constructed in the form of a Greek Cross." In the 1850s, the island boasted the Long Island Hotel, Long Island House, and the Eutaw House.

In response to the Civil War, the federal government seized a portion of Long Island Head for Fort Strong. By 1872, the hotels on the island became infamous for their illegal activities, ranging from prostitution to gambling and even cock fighting. Authorities raided the island in 1873 to shut down these so-called hotels of ill-repute.

The City of Boston purchased the island in 1882 and built a poor-house and eventually a chronic disease hospital. A home for unwed mothers and other asylums for those disenfranchised by society were also housed on the island. The facilities, menacing by design, included a crematorium for the hundreds of sick and suffering who perished in these reportedly inhumane facilities. Underground tunnels also connected the various buildings, some dating back to the Civil War.

Dennis Lehane, author of *Mystic River* and a Dorchester native, said the ghostly grounds of the sterile city hospital inspired his fictitious asylum-set novel *Shutter Island*, which was later turned into a movie by director Martin Scorsese. "My uncle took us out to Long Island once when my brother and I were kids," Lehane told the *Phoenix*. "He started telling us how the ghosts of the most dangerous patients were rumored to still walk the grounds. Then he vanished."

Lehane said the weathered structures scattered throughout the Long Island Chronic Disease Hospital inspired *Shutter Island*'s Ashecliffe Hospital for the Criminally Insane. "My brother and I walked around, all creeped out, and then my uncle jumped out from behind a tree, which gave us both early heart attacks. I remember it was just bleak and creepy," he recalled. "And that's all I needed to charge the battery for the book— bleak and creepy."

By 1928, homeless men and eventually women were housed on the island. Other treatment facilities for recovering addicts and alcoholics were eventually added. A bridge connecting Moon and Long Island was opened on August 4, 1951. For years, caregivers and patients were transported to Long Island by boats. However, the bridge was closed in October 2014 and destroyed in 2015.

When the rusty-old bridge closed, Long Island was completely evacuated. Camp Harbor View, a seasonal inner-city program spearheaded by the late Mayor Thomas Menino in 2007, is now the only sign of life left on an island once home to hundreds. Several cemeteries are located on the island, including the former hospital cemetery, which contains the remains of at least three thousand deceased patients.

Former residents of Long Island, many of whom stayed in the city's largest-run homeless shelter, said the island was definitely creepy. As the former editor of *Spare Change News*, I interviewed several of the homeless men and women who stayed there. Many believed it was haunted by the former patients of the chronic-disease hospital. "The only true nightmare on Long Island was being told that Mayor Marty Walsh had closed the bridge and the horrors we faced after we were carted off the island," said Cleve Rae, a formerly homeless man who recounted to me the inhumane treatment of hundreds of people forced off Long Island in October 2015.

I also chatted with young adults who stayed at Camp Harbor View. According to them, the Woman in Scarlet Robes is alive and well. In fact, the young campers' sleeping area is a stone's throw from Mary Burton's alleged makeshift grave. "I remember hearing about the ghost back in 2008," recalled an alum of Camp Harbor View. He asked to remain anonymous. "It scared the crap out of me. I remember hearing her moan and imagining this woman, covered in blood, hovering over me," he remembered. "I was so scared I slept with a flashlight on."

SPIRITS OF '76: HAUNTED FORTS

Do I think it's haunted? I would have to say yes, based on our EVP recordings.

—Anne Kerrigan, *Ghost Chronicles: Next Generation*

Peter Muise, author of *Witches and Warlocks of Massachusetts*, said there's something mysterious and oddly fascinating about Boston Harbor's series of forts. Many of these historic structures, he noted, are in an arrested state of decay, which only adds to their spooky mystique.

"Boston has a long history, and for many years was one of North America's most important port cities. The forts were built to defend the city from attacks by sea," he explained. "The first forts were built by the English to protect the city from enemies like the French, but also probably from random pirate attacks. When the American Revolution started, the British used the forts to control access to the harbor and as shelter from the Americans. After the Revolution the Americans used the forts to defend the city from the British in the War of 1812, and in the Civil War the forts helped protect Boston from attack by the Confederacy. Some of the harbor forts were also fitted with anti-aircraft guns during World War II."

As Boston's legends-and-lore expert, Muise said the forts dotting the islands of Boston Harbor are rich with stories, adding that a lot of the ghosts believed to be haunting the waters of Boston Harbor got their origins from real-life horrors. "Many traumatic events have happened on the islands," Muise continued. "Executions, massacres, shipwrecks, war, and deaths from disease. Some people believe traumas like those cause ghosts and other paranormal activities."

When it comes to haunted forts, Muise cited Edgar Allan Poe's memorable stint on South Boston's Fort Independence on Castle Island. The master of the macabre, who notoriously didn't like Boston, was born in the Bay Village and died in Baltimore, at age forty, in October 1849.

Poe had enlisted in the Army under the alias of Edgar A. Perry, claiming to be a clerk from Boston. While Poe reportedly wasn't happy with the homecoming, the Boston Harbor fort may have been the much-needed spark for one of his most popular stories.

According to Muise, the famous writer was looking for inspiration. "One day Poe noticed a gravestone in the fort's cemetery for a Lt. Robert Massie, who had died on December 25, 1817," he recalled. "After Poe commented on the misfortune of dying on a holiday, one of his fellow soldiers told him the tragic story behind Massie's death."

Massie was well liked by his peers at Fort Independence. However, one of his fellow officers, Gustavus Drane, had it in for the new recruit. Drane, an expert swordsman, argued with Massie over a card game on Christmas Eve. Drane challenged him to a duel and killed Massie on December 25, 1817. Yes, it was Christmas day.

"The enlisted men were outraged, and as they dug Massie's grave they quietly plotted how to avenge his death," continued Muise. "A few nights after the duel they put their plan into action. First, they invited Drane to come drink with them. Once he was heavily inebriated, they led him to an unused alcove inside the fort and chained him inside. Finally they walled up the alcove with bricks, sealing Drane inside forever."

According to lore, Poe was inspired by this real-life gruesome tale of revenge. Poe was discharged from Fort Independence in 1829, and the buried-alive story involving Drane was believed to be inspiration for his 1846 classic *The Cask of Amontillado,* where a man takes revenge on his drunken friend over an insult and ultimately entombs him alive.

Is the legend true? Muise said Poe did serve at Fort Independence but there is some debate about what really happened between Massie and Drane. A plaque at Fort Independence supposedly inspired Poe to dig for the backstory. Massie's remains were moved from Boston and reburied in Fort Devens. "It does appear that Massie was actually killed by Drane, but his killer was not entombed alive," continued Muise. "Instead Drane avoided a court martial, moved to Philadelphia, and got married. He died in 1846 at the age of fifty-seven."

However, a crew of Brown University archaeologists did find the remains of two charred human skeletons in the early 1900s. Also, folklorist Edward Rowe Snow claimed a skeleton wearing a military uniform buried in the bowels of Fort Independence was found in 1905.

In the Islands of Boston Harbor, Snow also wrote that Castle Island was cursed. According to pre–Revolutionary War legend, an English gentleman lived on the island with his daughter. The daughter had two suitors: One was British and had been picked by her father and the other was a colonist. She was smitten with the American boy, and the British man, enraged, challenged his competition to a duel. The Brit won, killing the young local. In a true *Romeo and Juliet* twist, the girl is said to have committed suicide in response to her lover's death. "The British officer, heartbroken, rushed down to the dock and plunged into the channel, crying he would put a curse on all who ever came near the island," wrote Snow. "Some sailors still believe that many shipwrecks near the Castle are to be blamed on this curse."

Snow said Castle Island was known for its bizarre suicides, including a man who jumped to his death in 1903 and a Somerville man who shot himself in the head in one of Fort Independence's casemates.

Of course, Castle Island isn't the only fort in Boston Harbor with a ghostly backstory. Muise also pointed out the many over-the-top urban myths swirling around this forgotten haunt nestled at the top of Hull Village's Telegraph Hill called Fort Revere.

Based purely on its weathered, graffiti tagged aesthetic, the fort looks like a typical ghost hangout. In fact, the long-deactivated fortification is buried in the ground and there are a series of labyrinthine tunnels and pitch-black hallways rumored to be haunted by the ghosts of its French prisoner-of-war past. Hundreds died from a smallpox outbreak in the late 1700s and some claim you can still hear a musical requiem echoing throughout its dark and scary halls.

Formerly called Fort Independence and renamed to honor minuteman Paul Revere, the earthen works battery has become a popular hangout for teens armed with cans of spray paint. Messages are sprayed throughout the fort. Some phrases are nonsensical, but the occasional wise one-liner, like "everything is hard before it is easy" and "welcome to the jungle," greets visitors to this once formidable haunt on the Hull peninsula.

Based purely on its breathtaking views, Fort Revere is the one spot in Boston Harbor where visitors can see the four Brewster islands and the majestic Boston Light in all its three-centuries-old glory. The Hull peninsula is also shouting distance from Peddocks Island, and the Pemberton Point ferry terminal is the closest people can get to the dock featured in Martin Scorsese's *Shutter Island* without actually taking a boat trip there during the summer.

During the American Revolution, Hull was the perfect location to view the real-life drama unfolding in Boston Harbor.

It's believed that Fort Revere was first occupied by rebel forces after the conclusion of George Washington's siege of Boston. In fact, historians believed the fort was used to fire on the British blockade in the harbor in June 1776. After the American Revolution, it was occupied by the French until 1780, who allied with the Patriot militia and sent military resources and an army to help fight the redcoats. During this era, the smallpox plague decimated those housed on Telegraph Hill. Fort Revere was reactivated during the War of 1812. The weathered fort that exists today was created in the late 1800s and became one of the various re-activated fortifications in Boston Harbor during World War I and World War II.

As far as the alleged hauntings at Fort Revere are concerned, the ghost lore sometimes overshadows its illustrious history.

"There have long been reports of whispering and the sound of footsteps in this abandoned U.S. military fort that is now a local tourist attraction," reported WZLX, a CBS-owned rock station. "Shadows pass under doorways as if people are walking past on the other side of the door, when there is actually no one there."

In 2013, a reporter with *Dig Boston* filed a story called "Unoccupied Boston: Fort Revere." Kat Strumm wrote that Fort Revere is "definitely haunted by bad graffiti artists" but was quick to dismiss the ghost lore associated with this Revolutionary War–era haunt. Strumm tested out the legends she deemed "lame" and conducted a mock investigation. Of course, she didn't encounter any paranormal activity.

"If you throw something in the tunnel, something might throw it back," Strumm recounted the legends. "If you stand still, you might see shadows with no source moving about. If you stand in a pitch-black room, of which there are many that smell like wet cigarettes and human pee, you can hear disembodied voices. Didn't happen for me."

In addition to its fortification history, the area known as Telegraph Hill was home to a communication tower built by John Rowe Parker in 1827. The first electrical telegraph came to Hull in 1853. Several other telegraph stations were built on the site and occupied the elevated location until 1938 when radio communications made the telegraph obsolete.

Anne Kerrigan, assistant director of East Bridgewater Community Television and co-host of *Ghost Chronicles: Next Generation,* told me she investigated Fort Revere with her now-disbanded paranormal team, East Bridgewater's Most Haunted, in 2007. Kerrigan believes there may be some truth behind the fort's over-the-top legends.

"We got a lot of EVPs here, one of which sounded like a choir singing," Kerrigan said, adding that she released the electronic-voice phenomenon on the show *East Bridgewater's Most Haunted*. "You will hear the EVP of the choir in this episode. We also heard the usual bumps and noises that were not accountable to anything directly," she continued.

Does Kerrigan think Fort Revere is haunted? Based on her five-hour investigation in 2007, she's not completely convinced. However, she was amazed by the EVPs captured by Michael Markowicz. "As far as anything specifically paranormal occurring when we were there, I would have to say no," she responded. "Do I think it's haunted? I would have to say yes, based on our EVP recordings."

Markowicz, who was interviewed by the *Patriot Ledger* about the investigation, said he didn't feel anything hostile at the investigation at Fort Revere. However, he was surprised by the singing captured on his digital recorder. Markowicz also recorded an EVP that oddly sounded as if his name was being repeated at a low frequency.

The disembodied male voice said: "What do you want with us, Michael?"

Watching the group's taped investigation, I found several of the EVPs unsettling. One voice said, "watch us, watch you," implying that the energy at the fort is possibly intelligent. Another voice responded to Kerrigan, on command, during one segment when she asked if the ghost was in the military. "I was a soldier," it responded. Kerrigan also conducted a pendulum session and the pendulum responded "yes" when asked if any female spirits reside at Fort Revere.

Oddly, the recording of the ghost choir of Fort Revere featured a female soprano singing a few notes from what sounded like an operatic aria. And yes, the ghostly opera singer was able to hit a few glass-shattering high notes.

Watch us, watch you? Perhaps they should change the name of the haunt in Hull to Fort Fear.

BETSY ROSS

When I visited Philadelphia in early November 2019, I stopped by the Betsy Ross House on Arch Street to pay my respect to America's most famous flag maker.

When I mentioned the trip to my historian friend, Bill Pavao, he said there's a lot of controversy surrounding the supposed historic landmark. "Betsy Ross was dug up and reburied in the yard in front of the property, however, that may not have been her house," Pavao told me. "So, she may be buried in the yard of a random stranger."

When I mentioned to Pavao that the Ross museum and gift shop is notoriously haunted, he joked that the otherworldly moans picked up by *Ghost Hunters* investigators in 2009 could be Ross making a postmortem plea to move her skeletal remains to a more appropriate location. "Maybe Betsy is hauntingly mad at being buried in someone else's yard?"

Even if Ross actually didn't live in the little house in the days leading up to the American Revolution, there's no denying her contribution to the cause. She stitched a flag with thirteen red-and-white stripes and stars, which cleverly represented the original colonies. Right?

Lisa Acker Moulder, the museum's executive director, told Steve Tawa from KYW Newsradio the original flag was "strictly utilitarian, used as a military tool," in an interview on July 2, 2019. "As a woman, she didn't have all the freedoms that others were afforded. This was her contribution to the founding of our country," Moulder added.

Of course, Moulder didn't mention what's known as the "Betsy Ross Myth."

In addition to rumors that the house wasn't actually Ross's property, there's a strong possibility she didn't actually sew the first American flag. Her story was told to the Historical Society of Pennsylvania and was relayed by her grandson, William Canby, in 1870. Yes, this bombshell was set off almost a century after the initial flag was supposedly crafted and wasn't even mentioned publicly during her lifetime.

The family member said his grandmother often recalled a visit she had in late May or early June of 1776 from the "flag committee," which included General George Washington and her relative, Colonel George Ross. Based on Canby's retelling, she was presented with a sketch of a flag and Ross added a few of her own personal touches to the design. Congress allegedly adopted her version on June 14, 1777, making the stars and stripes our national flag.

The story was picked up by *Harper's New Monthly Magazine* in 1873 and was soon viewed as fact and taught in elementary schools across the country. While historians can prove Ross did design flags, many believe the original was created by Francis Hopkinson, a New Jersey delegate to the Continental Congress and signer of the Declaration of Independence.

In fact, there was an invoice from Hopkinson in 1780 asking to be paid for the "flag of the United States of America." He was denied the money, however, from the Board of Admiralty because "he was not the only one consulted" on the design, which leaves the window open for Ross.

Did she or didn't she? I was unfazed by the controversy when I visited her home a few days after Halloween in 2019. When I walked into the gift shop and purchased a ticket to tour the property, I was told by the front desk staff that I would be able to ask Betsy Ross herself any questions I may have. Of course, they were referring to a reenactor.

I wanted to see for myself if there was any energy still lingering in the colonial-era home. As I walked through the museum, I did pass by the spot where Ross supposedly created the iconic flag. There was an inexplicable energy in the room, but it didn't become overwhelming until I headed downstairs into the basement.

I was anticipating a sweet, motherly figure. Not quite. The Ross reenactor was younger than I expected and a lot sassier. Apparently, the older woman who was featured in all of the advertisements plastered throughout the museum had the day off or was on break.

When I approached the performer, my first question for the in-character actress was about the reported ghosts haunting Ross's home. "I'm a Quaker so we don't believe in spirits," she shot back. "You're not going to find many spirits in Philadelphia."

I was shocked. No ghosts in the birthplace of our nation? I laughed.

The reenactor seemed annoyed by my questions related to the spirits associated with the house and tried to direct me out of the room. "Good luck on your journey," she said as she pointed to the exit sign.

I didn't even have a chance to ask her if she was upset that her family reinterred her remains in front of a house that probably wasn't her property. My takeaway from my brief-but-memorable visit: Don't cross Betsy Ross.

ROSS'S HAUNT: BETSY ROSS HOUSE

PHILADELPHIA, MA—When the former team from *Ghost Hunters* on Syfy visited the Betsy Ross House in 2009, they completely overlooked the possibility Ross may not have actually crafted the first American flag. The crew did, however, investigate the reported hauntings that have spooked the house museum's staff for years.

Lisa Acker Moulder, the organization's executive director, met with Grant Wilson and Jason Hawes from The Atlantic Paranormal Society (TAPS) outside of the property and talked about the various ghostly reports from her staff that included disembodied voices and what felt like a phantom hand touching their shoulder.

"I've heard lots of stories particularly from other directors," Moulder said, pointing to the museum. "This is the original house. We believe Betsy lived here between 1773 and 1775. It was during that time that she made the first American flag."

Wilson joked about the size of the building. "That was a huge flag to make in that little house," he said as the trio walked to Ross's gravesite outside of the property. "It was," Moulder responded. "And you can see her remains right here along with her third husband."

In addition to the historical significance associated with Ross's flag, Moulder explained there was a shooting in the basement of the museum's gift shop in the 1980s. "There was a scuffle between a couple of security guards," Moulder explained. "One of the security guards shot the other one three times and he left him overnight to die."

When asked if her employees experienced paranormal activity in the gift shop, Moulder nodded. "Some voices have been heard in the basement," she said. "Right above our cash registers is our loft space. That is where we keep the gift shop's backstock. It's loaded with boxes. A couple of weeks ago our staff heard boxes being moved up there when there was nobody there."

Saundra McDowell, a tour guide at the Betsy Ross House, recounted her experience with a shadow figure near the room where Ross supposedly met the flag committee. "I was sitting in the parlor and two dark shadows came by me," McDowell explained. "It felt like a presence. It just frightened me and it just kind of went by."

Moulder confirmed visitors to the museum have heard voices in the basement area of the Betsy Ross House. She then escorted the *Ghost Hunters* team to her office on the top floor of the museum, adding that the executive director's office is notoriously creepy.

"Our founder lived in this house until he died at the age of seventy-six. He actually died in this room from a stroke," Moulder said. "Some of the former directors have experienced things in this room. My predecessor was working late one night and was the only one on site and she was sitting at the computer. She felt a hand grasp her shoulder. The director before her was so freaked out about something that she climbed out of the window and onto the flagpole."

When Wilson asked if she had any idea why the previous director was so scared, Moulder said she didn't know.

During the *Ghost Hunters* investigation, the team heard phantom footsteps above them when they were investigating in the basement area. They also captured a ghostly conversation in the attic. The most convincing piece of evidence was an EVP of what sounded like a man saying, "Don't go."

They also heard a loud moan coming from the gift shop area. "It was loud enough that it radiated all the way down to the basement," Hawes told Moulder during the evidence reveal.

After presenting some convincing proof, Wilson was ambiguous in his analysis of the alleged hauntings. "This place is a great balance of potential activity and people who just love history in a unique building," he said. "You guys are very lucky here because you have a wonderful piece of history and have the chance to come face-to-face with history."

Moulder seemed visibly shocked when Wilson and Hawes presented the evidence. "I have to admit, I'm a little surprised because I was skeptical at the beginning of this process," she said. "The evidence that something has definitely occurred here really surprises me."

Even though Wilson captured a clear EVP of a man saying, "Don't go," he wasn't completely convinced that the Betsy Ross House was actually haunted. "I'm scratching my head because we had some activity but not enough to get anywhere," Wilson concluded.

MARY WASHINGTON

While George Washington's wife, Martha, faithfully supported her husband throughout his illustrious career, the first president's mother helped shape the man who successfully navigated the complexities of forming a new nation. Mary Ball Washington is often overlooked by history, but her strong-willed nature and work ethic was undeniably inherited by her oldest son.

Based on his famous quote honoring his mother, Washington recognized the woman who raised a family after her husband, Augustine, died prematurely in 1743 when George was only eleven years old. "My mother was the most beautiful woman I ever saw," Washington said. "All I am I owe to my mother. I attribute my success in life to the moral, intellectual, and physical education I received from her."

Washington became the man of the house once his father died. He helped his mother manage Ferry Farm, a thriving tobacco plantation in Virginia. As a young boy, Washington's father left him three prayer books. Currently stored at the Lyceum in Boston, the first president's mother inscribed her name in all three of the books.

Michelle Hamilton, manager of the Mary Washington House in Fredericksburg, Virginia, told me the matriarch had an often misunderstood bond with her famous son. "The relationship between George and Mary Washington has been left to speculation because only six letters that Mary wrote have survived," Hamilton said. "I would say it was a typical parent-and-child relationship in the eighteenth century in that it would have been formal and respectful."

For example, Washington addressed his mother as "Honour'd Madam" in his correspondence.

"This has led some historians to say they were not close," Hamilton said. "In the 1700s, the mother-and-son relationship would have been very formal, particularly with the gentry class. It was in the nineteenth century that the open expressions of maternal love became the norm in the relationships between parent and child."

Hamilton said that Mary groomed Washington to run his own plantation, however, he had bigger plans. "George decided he was going to follow a career in the military. As a parent, that made her very worried about his well-being," she said. "They were also very similar in temperament and were both very strong willed and stubborn. They both had a love for the outdoors that included riding horses and gardening. Because the two were so similar in temperament, they occasionally had disagreements."

In the three-part miniseries called *Washington* that premiered on the HISTORY Channel in February 2020, historians and modern-day leaders weighed in on the famous mother-and-son relationship.

"George Washington, like Barack Obama and Gerald Ford, was raised by a single mother. It's often overlooked how it impacted him," said Alexis Coe, author of *You Never Forget Your First: A Biography of George Washington*. "She was ambitious. She was savvy. She managed her estate very carefully. Washington wanted to live up to these values instilled in him by his mother."

General Colin Powell echoed Coe's comments. "Heaven knows how she handled all of that, but she did," Powell said. "She played such an important role in his life to give him the structure and confidence to believe in himself."

President Bill Clinton said in the *Washington* documentary that the founding father inherited a dogged determination from his mother, which was needed in his formative years. "He learned pretty early that he's going to have to depend upon himself," Clinton said. "I think he wanted to separate himself from his childhood and he had the strength and will to do it partly because he saw from his mother what it took to survive."

As Washington evolved into a leader, Hamilton said Mary became more nurturing. "As a whole, they had a very loving relationship," she said. "George publicly praised Mary and called her his 'revered mother.'

In 1789, George paid his mother a final visit before he went to New York to be sworn in. According to the family, he asked for her blessing, which she gave."

Mary lived to see her son command the Continental Army and lead the new country to independence. As Hamilton pointed out, Washington consulted with her in the days before he was inaugurated as the first president. He traveled from his home in Mount Vernon to visit his ailing mother dying from breast cancer in Fredericksburg, Virginia. Accompanied by Martha's grandson, George Washington Parke Curtis, he reconnected with the woman who raised him with a hard-headed realism needed to become a legendary commander-in-chief.

According to Curtis's account of the final meeting, Mary comforted her son from her deathbed. Washington planned to step away from public service, but his mother wanted him to assume his role as the nation's first leader. She said, "But go, George, fulfill the high destinies which Heaven appears to have intended for you. Go, my son, and may that Heaven's and a mother's blessing be with you always."

While her last words can't be verified, there's no denying she was proud of the accomplishments of her oldest child. Washington left Fredericksburg and was sworn in at New York City on April 30, 1789. His mother succumbed to cancer on August 25. She was eighty years old.

WASHINGTON'S HAUNT: MARY'S HOUSE

FREDERICKSBURG, VA—Not all hauntings are extreme. The namesake resident spirit of the Mary Washington House will speak up if something is out of place or an item in the gift shop goes against her personal beliefs. For the most part, however, she remains silent.

Apparently, the first president's mother doesn't like to make a scene even in the afterlife.

"We've had a couple paranormal groups investigate but there was nothing dramatic," reported Michelle Hamilton, the manager of the Mary Washington House and author of *Civil War Ghosts*. "Years ago a colonial lady was seen in the garden. We had to stop selling British toy soldier figurines in the gift shop because they would literally fly off the shelves. I've heard an occasional knock on the door and no one's there. We also hear people talking."

Hamilton admits that "It's very mild stuff, nothing scary at all."

The nation's first president purchased the white frame house on Charles Street in 1772 for his elderly mother. The property was close to Kenmore Plantation, which was where her daughter Betty Washington Lewis lived. Mary Ball Washington spent her golden years in the eighteenth-century home, hosting luminaries close to her famous son like the Marquis de Lafayette and Thomas Jefferson. She passed on August 25, 1789, after reportedly giving a blessing to her oldest child before he became president.

The property is currently a house museum and showcases artifacts from Washington's era including an antique mirror she called her "best dressing glass" and ceramics.

Like her son, Mary was opinionated and her strong-willed point of view has psychically imprinted itself into the walls of her home. Hamilton said Mary constantly worried about the well-being of her child especially during his early days in the military.

"As a youth, Washington was sickly and also she knew he could be reckless," Hamilton explained. "After his first battle, he wrote home that there was something charming about the sound of bullets whipping past. That was enough to give any mother the vapors."

Joni Mayhan, an author and paranormal investigator, said the subtle hauntings reported at the Mary Washington House are consistent with the matriarch's personality during life. "Not all ghosts are the maniacal, malicious entities people often imagine," Mayhan told me. "Some of them retain their gentle, congenial personalities after death and have no need to lash out at the living. They simply want to continue residing at their former homes and don't wish to be bothered. If someone draws their interest, they might provide a modest sign of their presence, but it usually comes infrequently and isn't blatant enough to generate attention."

Mayhan believes that out of all of the reported paranormal activity reported in the Mary Washington House, the redcoat soldier figurines being pushed off the shelves in the gift shop was significant. "Sometimes there will be a change in their former home that brings them out of their quiet existence," she said. "Mary Washington didn't want her son, George, to go to war and probably resents seeing British soldier figurines inside her own home. By knocking them to the floor, she let it be known they needed to be removed. For her, it probably felt like provocation."

As a medium, Mayhan said she often encounters ghosts lurking in places where people are unaware of them. "They hang back in the corners or reside in attics and basements where they are left alone. They have no need to draw attention to themselves," Mayhan said. "They just want to be where they are."

Mayhan said she completely understands Washington's postmortem plea. "As a mother, I wouldn't want my son to go to war either," she said. "She wanted to keep him home and keep him safe."

Cheri Lynn, also a medium and paranormal investigator, agreed with Mayhan. "I believe we retain our personalities when we pass away," Lynn said. "This includes emotions, preferences, sense of humor, anxieties, and fears. I believe our soul permeates every cell in our bodies. When we die, the soul continues but is transformed into a spirit state."

Lynn said it's common for spirits to remain at the place of their death or return to a location they're familiar with like their former home. "Their personality or state of mind at the time of death, I believe, can determine the level or type of activity observed," Lynn said. "In either situation, the soul may only make their presence known when they are unhappy with changes to their environment, things that are happening that they don't agree with or when they want to be included in life events."

In other words, Washington's mother may be expressing her anti-war sentiment from the other side. When asked if the toy soldiers from the Continental Army were also knocked off the shelves in the gift shop, the museum's manager said no. "The Patriots stayed on the shelf," Hamilton told me. "We figured the house's spirit disliked the redcoats and I asked for them not to be restocked."

PETER SALEM

History has overlooked the contributions of thousands of African-American soldiers who valiantly fought on both sides of the Revolutionary War. Enslaved men signed on with either the Patriots or the British hoping their service will ultimately result in freedom. Unfortunately, it didn't pay off for a majority of the enlisted men of color.

"Historians estimate between 5,000 and 8,000 African-descended people participated in the Revolution on the Patriot side, and upward of 20,000 served the crown," reported Colette Coleman on History.com. "Many fought with extraordinary bravery and skill, their exploits lost to our collective memory."

Liberty and justice for all apparently didn't apply to the black men who fought in the American Revolution. Slavery was abolished in 1804 by the northern states and the practice continued until Congress adopted the 13th Amendment as part of the U.S. Constitution on December 18, 1865.

Meanwhile, enlisted soldiers of color like Peter Salem emerged as heroes of the War of Independence. Born into slavery in Framingham, Massachusetts, Salem was sold to Lawson Buckminster who became a major in the Continental Army. He gave Salem his freedom in 1775 so he could join the local militia.

Salem became a valuable asset during the war's first battles at Concord, Massachusetts, on April 19, 1775, and later at the Battle of Bunker Hill. It's believed Salem fatally shot one of the conflict's key British soldiers, Major John Pitcairn, as he was climbing to the top of the American redoubt demanding a surrender from the rebel soldiers. If Salem was actually responsible for the killing, then his courageous efforts were memorialized in John Trumbull's famous painting, *The Battle of Bunker's Hill.*

He also fought in two later battles in Saratoga and Stony Point and then retired from the military in 1780. Salem married and built a cabin in Leicester, Massachusetts, spending his peaceful, post-war life as a cane weaver. Salem died on August 16, 1816. He was sixty-six years old.

The hero was interred in the Old Burying Ground in Framingham, which is a stone's throw from one of the Bay State's most haunted cemeteries known locally as The Rev because of its numerous Revolutionary War graves, including veterans Elijah McIntire, Jonathan Page, and Joseph Polley.

"The Dean Hill Cemetery is rife with legend," said author Joni Mayhan. "Located down a long, narrow dead-end road, the stage is set far before you arrive at your destination."

Mayhan told me people who visit the cemetery have heard blood-curdling screams. "Some say satanic rites were performed in the woods surrounding the desolate cemetery, causing the area to become deadly quiet for several years," she said. "People who visited were so unnerved by the absence of insect, bird, and animal sounds, they left shortly afterwards."

Several deaths have occurred in the area, including a boy who supposedly burned to death and a woman who died in a car accident near the entrance. Two teens reportedly disappeared after becoming frightened in the cemetery. When they raced to their car, it wouldn't start, so they fled on foot, never to be seen again.

In 1882, Framingham built a monument to honor Salem's contributions during the American Revolution. The memorial is next to his grave at the Old Burying Ground on Main Street off Buckminster Square.

SALEM'S HAUNT: BUNKER HILL

CHARLESTOWN, MA—Bunker Hill, which is actually Breed's Hill in Charlestown, has a rather mixed-up history. The pivotal Revolutionary War battle on June 17, 1775, would be considered a comedy of errors if it didn't result in hundreds of deaths. Yes, the revisionist history of the legendary battle in Charlestown is basically bunk.

"The whole thing's a screw-up," said *Bunker Hill* author Nathaniel Philbrick in *Smithsonian* magazine. "The Americans fortify the wrong hill, this forces a fight no one planned, the battle itself is an ugly and confused mess. And it ends with a British victory that's also a defeat."

While the British technically won, their death toll was 226 coupled with more than 800 wounded redcoats. The colonists, in comparison, had 115 fatalities and 305 wounded soldiers. Yes, the British won the Battle of Bunker Hill, but the Patriots' stubborn resistance became a symbol of the American resolve.

The whole "don't fire until you see the whites of their eyes" statement, supposedly issued by Israel Putnam to the Patriots, was probably made up as well. But it's emblematic of the confusion associated with Bunker Hill. When you have this sort of chaos coupled with hundreds of fatalities, it leaves what paranormal investigators call an aura of disaster. And in this highly-charged environment, it's a perfect storm for ghosts.

When I interviewed psychic MaryLee Trettenero in 2013, she talked about her residual-energy readings on Breed's Hill. According to Trettenero's book *We're Still Here*, she connected with the spirits on the land next to the Bunker Hill Monument. She read the residual energy and claimed to have connected with a Patriot preparing for battle. The spirit talked about "rotting flesh," and Trettenero surmised that it was related to the casualties from the British warship *Lively*, which killed several Patriots with cannonballs. One soldier was decapitated while others lost limbs and three were literally ripped apart by the shrapnel.

Of course, this happened before the face-to-face combat on Breed's Hill, which meant an actual skirmish took place before the battle. In her book, Trettenero said she psychically replayed the horrors of that hot June day by reading the residual energy at Breed's Hill. "One by one, we are falling. We drop right in our tracks," the spirit told her. "The wounded have no distinction from the dead. We are in a holocaust. British uniforms are conveying blood."

According to Trettenero, the battle left a psychic imprint on the land. "Not all remains were removed," Trettenero wrote. "Since the British took over control of Breed's Hill, some of the fallen soldiers were buried in shallow graves. When the British left on Evacuation Day, March 17, 1776, the provincial army returned to Charlestown to reclaim the soldiers who had been buried at the site of the battle so they could have a proper burial."

Paranormal experts believe the residual hauntings Trettenero is picking up on are psychic remnants of the killings and unmarked graves leftover from the almost 250 years of bloodstained soil still left from the Battle of Bunker Hill.

And, apparently, not all of the bodies left to rot on Breed's Hill were given an acceptable final resting spot.

In 2009 a group of archeologists and a Charlestown historian Chris Anderson located a mass grave of British soldiers beneath a residential garden near Monument Square's Concord Street. "No wonder our plants grow so well," mused Anne McMahon, a Charlestown resident, when she was told by a *Boston Globe* reporter about the mass grave beneath her rose bushes. "They're resting in peace. They're not haunting the place and we wish them well. It's all peaceful now. I guess that's what we were fighting for."

In addition to the skeletal secrets buried beneath Breed's Hill, there's the iconic Bunker Hill Monument, which also has a somewhat bizarre history. The cornerstone of the obelisk was laid in 1825, and famous orator Daniel Webster addressed a crowd of one hundred thousand there. Eight-ton granite blocks were transported from a quarry south of Boston. However, money ran out. Sarah Josepha Hale, author of "Mary Had a Little Lamb" and a magazine editor, organized a "Ladies' Fair," which raised $30,000 to save the half-built structure. Eighteen years after the initial ceremony, an aged Webster returned in 1843 to announce its dedication.

It's common for visitors to the Bunker Hill Monument to take photos of orbs near the 221-foot granite structure. But are these orbs actually ghosts from Charlestown's past?

Adam Berry, a paranormal investigator from *Kindred Spirits*, told me he's wary of so-called orbs presented to him in photos. "Most of the time it's just dust or insects," he explained. "The definition of an orb is a spherical object that produces its own light. So a real orb is created naturally by energy, or in theory, it's a spirit floating through and trying to show itself to you."

Berry continued: "If you take a picture, especially outside, sometimes the flash will reflect off dust or insects, and while they look round, they're not giving off their own light. Say it's next to a tree and it's a real orb, the tree would be illuminated by this object. In Gettysburg, for example, I've seen orbs that give off their own light, and they are completely different from dust."

People who have visited Gettysburg echo Berry's comments regarding the difference between real orbs at battlefields and light anomalies commonly captured in photos.

Does this mean the orb photos shot at Bunker Hill are actually legit? Trettenero said she's a believer. In fact, she claimed to have had spirit encounters with Webster near the obelisk and even picked up on the residual chatter of people talking about his famous oration.

FORGOTTEN SPIRITS OF '76

Ghosts don't scare me. People scare me.
                    —Joe "Jiggy" Webb, paranormal investigator

When I was interviewed by talk show host Bradley Jay in October 2019, I was able to solve a mystery that has haunted the WBZ radio personality for years: *Who was Black Mark?*

Jay had asked other local authors and historians on his late-night podcast and they had no clue what he was talking about. "I heard indirectly that there was a man who was hanged in Boston Common and was laid there to rot for four years," he said. "All I remembered was his name was Black Mark."

While the location of Jay's story was incorrect, Mark's tragic backstory was shockingly true.

"It was horrific," I said on the live broadcast of his *Jay Talking* radio show. "This was in 1755, years after the Salem witch trials, and Mark wasn't hanged in Boston, but in Cambridge of all places. Mark, along with a woman named Phillis, was accused of murdering a slave owner. They took his body and put it into a gibbet cage, which was a crude contraption designed by the Puritans as a public reminder of his crime."

During the eighteenth century, the case was well known. In fact, Paul Revere mentioned Mark in the account of his famous midnight ride on April 18, 1775. The enslaved duo and supposed co-conspirators, however, were somehow forgotten by history.

"It's surprising to me that we don't talk about this story because it's such a horrible way to execute someone," I said on the radio show. "What is even more tragic is that Mark and Phillis were probably innocent of killing Captain Codman. They were scapegoats in my opinion."

I first heard about the tragic story when I interviewed Gavin W. Kleespies, former director of the Cambridge Historical Society, in 2013.

"Mark and Phillis, two slaves accused of poisoning Captain John Codman, a Charlestown merchant whose 'rigid discipline' they had found 'unendurable,' were executed," Kleespies recounted in the historical society's newsletter. "Phillis, as was customary, was strangled and her body burned. Mark was hanged and his body suspended in irons on a gibbet along what is now Washington Street in Somerville, near the Charlestown line."

When Paul Revere rode past the gibbet cage twenty years after the hanging, Mark's decomposed body became a literal landmark for the minuteman. "After I had passed Charlestown Neck, and got nearly opposite where Mark was hung in chains, I saw two men on horseback, under a tree," Revere recalled. "When I got near them, I discovered they were British officers."

Mark was hanged in Cambridge and then tarred and gibbeted in an iron cage near the present-day Holiday Inn on Somerville's Washington Street. According to one unnamed colonial-era physician, the tar used to preserve the body had surprisingly worked and the doctor wrote that Mark's "skin was but little broken altho' he had been hanging there for nearly three or four years."

Apparently, the "Black Mark" moniker wasn't referring to the color of the executed man's skin, but the black tar used to keep his corpse intact. Phillis, on the other hand, was savagely strangled and then burned at the stake.

And, yes, this tragedy has psychically imprinted itself in the environment.

According to local sources, many of the homes and former Lesley College buildings surrounding the execution site are teeming with the tortured spirits from Cambridge's Gallows Hill past.

"Phenomena include disembodied footsteps and objects that move by themselves," wrote Dennis William Hauck in *Haunted Places: The National Directory*. Also, the *Boston Globe* reported Phillis's cries can be heard echoing throughout Avon Hill. "They say, if you listen closely on a windy day, you can still hear her screaming as she went up in smoke," said tour guide Daniel Berger-Jones.

In addition to the inexplicable sounds and shadows, there are reports of a female specter wearing colonial-era attire, weeping and sometimes shrieking. Adam Berry from the Travel Channel's *Kindred Spirits* said it's possible the residual energy surrounding the Gallows Hill site is left behind from the public executions. In the past, Berry said he's heard "reports of women wailing or crying. They're in grief. It's possible something traumatic has happened and they've died or they're searching for their son or soldier."

Or perhaps it's Phillis posthumously begging for justice and setting the record straight about the man she and Mark may—or may not—have murdered with arsenic.

While researching the Mark and Phillis case in 2013, I was mysteriously drawn to the oldest structure in Cambridge, the Cooper-Frost-Austin House on Linnaean Street. It's open once a year, in June, and my intuition led me to the little white building tucked away in North Cambridge's Avon Hill. The lean-to "half house" was built by Samuel Cooper, a deacon of First Church in the early eighteenth century, and was passed down the Cooper family tree for 250 years.

The historic home is a stone's throw from Cambridge's Gallows Hill. And, yes, that's the spot where Mark and Phyllis were executed.

While dozens of people were hanged near the property during the colonial era, the spirit haunting the Cooper-Frost-Austin House passed in 1885. According to Brian Powell, the structure's year-round resident and tour guide, he's heard several stories from former tenants who claim the ghost of the last owner, Susan Austin, still lingers in the upstairs bedroom.

"I was checking out a book at the Boston Public Library and the librarian recognized my address as the Cooper-Frost-Austin House. He said he lived here for a week and would never go back," Powell told me.

Why? "He said it was haunted. He was literally spooked and spent a week in this house in complete terror. People speculate it's the last owner, Susan Austin, but I've never encountered her," Powell said, joking that he's comfortable sharing a home with the female specter. "I don't care if she's here. You can be dead as long as you don't bother me when I'm sleeping," he said. "But I've been approached by psychics and others who believe the house is active."

As far as my baseline sweep of the oldest building in Cambridge, I did spot what looked like a shadow figure dart across the downstairs in the main hall, which boasts original masonry detail in the fireplaces and the foot of the structure's chimney dating back to 1681.

During the tour, a hanging lamp mysteriously started to sway when we were in the original kitchen area, and when our small group toured the haunted upstairs bedroom, eerily in a state of arrested decay, we heard inexplicable phantom footsteps creaking above us in the attic. Apparently, the third floor is where the servants stayed. In the past, I've spotted what looked like a full-bodied apparition of a woman, lit by candlelight, peeking from the window of the second-floor bedroom when I've walked down Linnaean Street.

The weekend before my visit to the Hooper-Lee-Nichols House, I was asked a question while giving one of my ghost tours that really baffled me: Why were all of the spirits featured on my historical-based ghost tours in Boston mostly "white men with money?"

I was stumped. I couldn't think of one story during our walk through Boston's haunted cemeteries and cobblestone streets that featured a person of color. The question inspired me to dig a little deeper for the skeletal secrets hidden in the city's Revolutionary War–era closet.

Of course, Boston isn't alone in its lack of representation in the spirit realm. Author Tiya Myles expertly explored the topic in *Tales from the Haunted South*. "Black history had all been ignored at historic homes and plantation sites," she wrote in her book, which was inspired by a visit to Savannah, Georgia. "The people who had mattered in these tours were the slave-holding high society families, not their chattel slaves."

Paranormal investigator Joe "Jiggy" Webb echoed a similar sentiment when I interviewed him in 2013. Back then, Webb wanted to give a voice to those historically marginalized and he believed paranormal-themed programs lacked diversity.

Webb's critique? Enough already with the familiar haunts revisited over and over again on television.

"The problem with these shows is they do the same thing," he said during our visit to Cambridge's Old Burying Ground. "They go to the same places. We know the Lizzie Borden house is probably haunted. Why do they keep going there? There's got to be a million other places throughout the country with a lot of history."

The paranormal investigator said there's a lack of diversity at these supposedly haunted locales and little to no representation of people of color on ghost-hunting TV shows. "Here in New England, we have so much history," he remarked. "You can't tell me all of that history is outside of Roxbury, Dorchester, and Mattapan."

As far as Cambridge, he said he wants to leave no gravestone unturned when he investigates a supposedly haunted location. "It's a beautiful city," Webb said. "It's very diverse. I grew up in the

South End and would come into Harvard Square all the time, and I was interested in the history here."

Webb said he had his first face-to-face encounter with a ghost when he was seven years old. He saw a full-bodied apparition of a man who introduced himself and then disappeared. "It wasn't like it was a reflection in a mirror," he recalled. "Clearly, it was like somebody standing right in front of me." The investigator said he later recognized the spirit from a photograph: it was his grandfather, who passed away before Webb was born.

"It was definitely him," he insisted. "I mean, my house in the South End was haunted. My house in Brockton was also haunted to the point everyone in my family knew it was haunted."

Webb said his interest in the paranormal rekindled after a series of near-death experiences, or "NDEs," as he calls them. "I was always into it, but it just seemed so abnormal," he said. In 2003, he was shot in the leg and then walked away from a totaled car with just a bruise.

It was his recent brush with mortality in 2006, however, that opened his so-called third eye. "I had a brain aneurysm that burst, and I ended up having brain surgery," he said. "It was extremely profound. It was so profound that I came back a different person. My beliefs, my understanding, my thought processes weren't the same."

Webb, who operated a security firm during the day, said he immersed himself in all things paranormal after the surgery. "People think you're crazy when you start talking outside of the box," he said. "But when your brain explodes and you're trying to explain it to somebody else, it isn't the easiest thing. So I started coming out of my shell and began talking to people about it."

In 2011, he organized a team of paranormal investigators called HooDeez. Webb then launched an online radio show, *Paranormal Hood*, which included a series of TV webisodes chronicling the team's investigations at sites like Somerville's Prospect Hill. "I started reaching out to people who didn't think I was crazy, and then we started doing investigations," Webb said. "On many investigations, strangers walk up to us and participate. You can sit at home and watch these investigations or you can do them yourself," he continued.

Webb's plan of attack? "They always go to the same places and do the same things on these shows," he said. "Branch out.

Do something original. There are so many things out there that haven't been explored."

The ghost hunter said it's important to embrace diversity and to investigate hauntings in communities of color. "What we talk about to ourselves and what we talk about to other people are two different things," he said, referring to the African-American culture. "When you bring somebody from the outside, they're probably not going to talk. We like getting the public involved. We like turning skeptics into believers. People are like, 'We don't believe in ghosts,' and then they completely change their minds after going on an investigation with us. It's the thrill of the hunt."

During the day, Webb has worked as a bodyguard for stars like Faith Evans, Naughty by Nature, and Gavin DeGraw. When asked if ghost hunting is like chasing celebrities, he laughed. "I don't chase celebrities. I bodyguard them," he told me. "I've met very few celebrities who are nice. So if you want to liken them to ghosts, there are bad ghosts and there are bad celebrities. If you're chasing celebrities, you're chasing something you want. I don't want to come back as a ghost. I don't want to haunt my family."

As far as local investigations, Webb said he was unnerved during a tour of Somerville's Prospect Hill. "I've been on many investigations, and this one definitely spooked me," he says, referring to a scene from the *Paranormal Hood* show where he's standing in front of the historic castle and feels something from beyond touch him. "It could have been a bug, but something makes me jump. I felt like something grabbed me."

Webb said, however, he's less creeped out by spirits and more wary of the living. "I've been shot and I've been stabbed. That was all done by living people," he said. "Ghosts don't scare me. People scare me."

In an attempt to give a voice to New England's ghosts who have been historically marginalized by the status quo, I reached out to MaryLee Trettenero. The psychic and author has the ability to connect with the lingering residual energy at a haunted location and then channels the earth-bound spirits.

Trettenero, who moved to Charlestown in the 1980s, said she was standing on the steps of Harvard's Widener Library, while taking classes at the extension school, when she decided to leave the hotel industry and become a full-time psychic medium. "I haven't told many people this, but this is where I made the decision to go into the business," she said. "Once I left working in hotels, it was the only thing that really interested me. I started at a good time because it's so difficult now. The [psychic field] has become so competitive."

In 2005, Trettenero decided to redirect her intuitive abilities and channel the residual energy at historic locations. "My premise is if I can read people, then I should be able to go to a place and read the land," she said. "If energy from a historic event is strong, it stays there." As for reading potentially haunted locations, Trettenero said it's a two-fold process. "First, I pick up on the residual historical energy. The second thing is if there is spirit energy there, I would pick up on the spirits," she explained, adding that "it was a big experiment. I didn't know if it was going to work."

Trettenero said her first attempt at reading residual energy was at City Square Park in Charlestown. "I sat in the middle of the foundation of stones, and I started picking up on slave girls," she recalled. "I got dialogue and what it was like working back then and what it was like dealing with the proprietors. So I would visit the site, do some protection, and then tune in. Another time, I picked up on a bartender, and one time I picked up on a pirate. After reading a place, I go back and do research and find it's often so true to form. I'm finding that what I get from the fragments I pick up at a site is historically accurate. It fits."

City Square Park in Charlestown, which was originally called Market Square, dates back to 1629. Governor John Winthrop and his crew of one thousand English settlers originally set up shop there before sniffing around Cambridge and ultimately Boston. Thomas Graves, an English engineer, mapped out Charlestown and built Winthrop's quarters, called the Great House, in the area before relocating to Boston's Shawmut Peninsula in 1630.

The square was destroyed when British cannon fire burned Charlestown to the ground on June 17, 1775. Trettenero said she tapped into a residual energy that lingers at City Square Park and predates the Battle of Bunker Hill fire.

"So when I picked up on the slave girls, I researched the slavery background and John Winthrop moving to Charlestown, and I found that slavery was totally integrated into society," she explained. "The last owner before City Square Park was burned to the ground was a slave owner."

Trettenero said she sometimes picks up on ghosts while researching historical sites. "A few days ago, I was at the Warren Tavern having lunch," she said, referring to the haunted watering hole in Charlestown built in 1780. "I was with a friend, chit chatting, and all of sudden the lights started flickering behind me. She makes me stop talking and asks, 'Who is that?' I stopped what I was doing and tuned into it. I could see somebody wearing a black coat and he was severe looking. I immediately knew who it was—it was Daniel Webster. As soon as I said his name, my friend who is a colleague said his name popped up into her mind as well."

How does Trettenero differentiate among the various spirits she encounters during investigations? "I have a sketch artist who works with me," she explained, adding that she first encountered Daniel Webster's spirit at the Bunker Hill Monument. "We do sketches of the spirits we see, and that's why I know what he looks like."

Trettenero managed to assemble her residual-energy readings into a book format called *We're Still Here: The Secret World of Bunker Hill's Historical Spirits*, which came out in 2015. "Years ago, I put it in the format of a book, but I put it down because it wasn't in a language that was easy to edit. I then added layers, like adding a sketch artist, and then I started working on paranormal investigations."

Trettenero, who operates a ghost tour in Charlestown, said the city is a hotbed of residual energy. "A lot of my stuff is related to the American Revolution," she said. "I do know that the guy Harvard is named after, John Harvard—his original home is one of the sites I do in Charlestown. It's not there anymore, but what I found is that it was a medical staging area. I just picked up on dialogue around it regarding clean water and arguments about who they are going to treat, specifically wounded British soldiers and people of color."

Trettenero continued, "Charlestown was burned to the ground during the Revolutionary War. But I strongly believe the medical staging was there before the war because there was a lot of violence before the Battle of Bunker Hill."

The spirits of enslaved girls lingering in Charlestown's City Square Park? I was getting closer to a more accurate backstory of what really went down in the years leading up to the American Revolution.

Our country's history is full of secrets.

"By 1775 more than a half-million African Americans, most of them enslaved, were living in the thirteen colonies," wrote historian Edward Ayres on the American Revolution Museum at

Yorktown's website. "Widespread talk of liberty gave thousands of slaves high expectations, and many were ready to fight for a democratic revolution that might offer them freedom. In 1775 at least ten to fifteen black soldiers, including some slaves, fought against the British at the battles of Lexington and Bunker Hill. By 1776, however, it had become clear that the revolutionary rhetoric of the founding fathers did not include enslaved blacks."

In the early drafts of the Declaration of Independence, for example, Thomas Jefferson changed the semantics from "all men are born equally free" to "all men were created equal" to prevent the idea that enslaved men and women should be free.

Yes, human trafficking was a hot-button topic in the years leading up to the American Revolution and the subject would rear its ugly head during the Civil War less than one century later.

In 1772, the British courts issued a landmark court decision that involved a runaway slave, James Somerset, who fled his owner Charles Stewart in Boston. The abolitionist movement overseas sided with the enslaved man in the *Somerset vs. Stewart* case and the courts decided that "slavery was antithetical to the British constitution and English common law."

This ruling wasn't enforced in America and the colonists—especially in the southern region—were afraid the Somerset case would be a threat to their growing agrarian economy.

While there were many factors that fueled the War of Independence, there's no denying our young country's reliance on slavery was one of them. With a continued emphasis on the more progressive founding fathers like Benjamin Franklin and John Adams, our nation has a history of forgetting its dark past, which includes the barbaric executions of Mark and Phillis.

Sadly, America was built on the backs of slaves and its land is stained with their blood.

TOWN CRIER Q&A: JONI MAYHAN

The Revolutionary War was a traumatic event for those who lived it. Even after they died, they couldn't let go of that devastation and injustice.

—Joni Mayhan, *Ghost Magnet*

Want a room with a "boo" in Massachusetts where the "shot heard round the world" was fired? Joni Mayhan, author of *Ghost Magnet* and *Dark and Scary Things,* recommends Concord's Colonial Inn near Minute Man National Park.

Built in 1716, the overnight haunt is located just down the road from the North Bridge, where the Battles of Lexington and Concord occurred. The historic inn is wicked haunted according to Mayhan.

"Imagine waking up in the middle of the night to find a Revolutionary War soldier standing at the foot of your bed," she told me. "During the Revolutionary War, a portion of the inn was used to store firearms and provisions for the militia. Another section was the office of Dr. Thomas Milot. Wounded soldiers were brought to his office during the battle, and many succumbed to their injuries, lending truth to the ghostly encounters."

Converted to an inn around 1889 and renamed Concord's Colonial Inn eleven years later, the hotel was home to Henry David Thoreau, famous for his "Civil Disobedience" essay and, of course, *Walden.* Thoreau lived in the inn while he attended Harvard. The eighteenth-century structure served as a boarding house before being transformed into a hotel called the Thoreau House, named after the famous writer's aunts.

"When I had the opportunity to investigate the inn years ago, I wasn't disappointed by the activity," Mayhan said. "While we didn't see the soldier materialize in the bedroom, we did witness strange tapping sounds, shadows moving, and odd smells appearing out of nowhere. While conducting an EVP session in an attempt to get the resident ghosts to speak to us through our digital recorders, a lacy doily flew off the back of a chair and landed on my head, surprising me."

In the interview, Mayhan talked about her connection with the spirits lingering at Concord's Colonial Inn and weighed in on the types of hauntings associated with the American Revolution.

In some cases, history repeats itself—over and over again—in an endless ghost loop.

Q: Are the ghosts associated with the American Revolution more residual or intelligent based on your experience?
A: War is a violent affair. It changes the vibration of a landscape and alters its energetic composition, leaving it vastly different than it was before the horrors began. Even though many of the souls who fought and died in the battle crossed over and continued their spiritual journeys, many others remained. Some of them didn't realize they were dead, wandering around the battlefields looking for their battalions. Others stayed to look after loved ones or homes they cherished.

As time passed, I believe many of the earthbound souls eventually found their way to Heaven, but the land didn't forget. The memory of all those lost lives and the devastation of war leached into the ground, leaving a spiritual wound behind.

Q: What exactly is a residual haunting?
A: Residual energy is a memory kept by the land itself. When extreme trauma occurs in an area, it becomes absorbed into the energy field of the location. We know everything on our planet vibrates. A higher vibration is one that exists harmonically with all

that surrounds it. It draws in other high vibrational frequencies, much like metal fragments being pulled to a magnet.

Events such as tragic death, battles, and extreme violence lowers the vibration of an area, turning something lovely and tranquil into a seething pot of angst, anguish, and sometimes hatred. This also draws complementary energy, pulling in additional lower vibrational frequencies until the land is nearly saturated with it.

In most residual hauntings, an event is played out over and over again. A company of soldiers might be spotted in a foggy field, marching out to battle, even though the souls of these soldiers crossed over to Heaven long ago. If you tried to communicate with the soldiers, you wouldn't have success, because they aren't really there. What you are seeing is similar to a projection flashed upon a huge screen. It's the memory of a moment caught in time.

Q: During your investigation of Concord's Colonial Inn, what type of spirits did you encounter?
A: I investigated the Concord Colonial Inn early in my paranormal career. I had just latched onto my metaphysical gifts and was experimenting with them, much like a kid with a new toy. Thankfully, I was there with several paranormal veterans, including a talented psychic medium and several experienced mediums.

The ghost I remember the clearest was the soul of a Revolutionary War soldier. Guests of the inn have witnessed this soldier walking into their room in the middle of the night. They see him as a wispy apparition in shades of black and white. After he comes into the room, he stands at the foot of the bed before dissipating into thin air. This was the first room we investigated.

There were five of us scattered around the room. We dimmed the lights, turned on our digital recorders, and sat silently for a moment. The room buzzed with paranormal energy. You could feel it hanging in the air like a current of electricity.

When he drifted in, I felt him immediately.

Q: Were you able to communicate with the Revolutionary War soldier?
A: We attempted to communicate with the ghost and received a faint response on our digital recorder. We asked if he was a soldier and he said, "Yes." The rest of our questions went unanswered, but that didn't mean we didn't glean information. The mediums in our group continued writing for the duration of the session. Once the session ended, I asked them to read what they sensed.

Every one of us picked up on the fact he was a soldier. This wasn't surprising because we came into the room with this one piece of information. What interested me were the descriptions. We didn't know what he looked like prior to the investigation. We only knew he presented himself in shades of black and white. Every single medium described him as having dark blond hair that was longish and unkempt. Three out of the five of us saw him with a head wound, one that probably took his life, and we all were certain he wasn't aware he was dead.

With this knowledge, we attempted to cross him over, but he refused to go. He was still trapped in the battle, intent on finishing his mission. He dismissed us and promptly disappeared into the night.

Q: Any idea why Concord's Colonial Inn is so haunted?
A: I believe the haunting of the Concord Colonial Inn is primarily due to the residual energy effect. There were countless traumas that happened in the area, resulting in horrific deaths. Emotions also played a tremendous role. People fought hard for what they believed in, and they gave their lives for the cause. The land recorded this event, providing residual energy, while the earth-bound souls remained there, reliving their deaths over and over again.

Q: Can locations like Concord's Colonial Inn become more haunted over time?
A: Yes. Places where ghosts are known to linger become almost a weigh station for other ghosts who are drawn there by the spiritual energy. The original haunting was probably focused around the Revolutionary War, but over time others have joined the colony.

As we investigated, we discovered a young woman in a hallway who hailed from the 1960s time period. She was distraught and emotional and wasn't interested in talking with us. We also found a young boy and an older man in the kitchen, neither of whom were tied to the Revolutionary War period.

Q: Based on your experience, why do spirits from the Revolutionary War still linger?
A: The Revolutionary War was a traumatic event for those who lived it. If you try to understand their mindset during that time period, it makes more sense. These people broke away from a country that

didn't allow them free reign to live their lives. They endured horrific conditions and harrowing experiences to get to the new world,
only to have someone threaten to take it all away from them.
Many of them lost loved ones, homes, and their sense of security.
Even after they died, they couldn't let go of that devastation and
injustice. Many of them are still fighting for a freedom we've been
enjoying for more than two hundred years.

THE
LOYALISTS

Independence Hall in Philadelphia, Pennsylvania, is where both the United States Declaration of Independence and the United States Constitution were debated and adopted. *Courtesy Deposit Photo*

BENEDICT ARNOLD

The word *traitor* has been synonymous with Benedict Arnold, however, there's no denying the former merchant from Connecticut got a bum rap before he committed the ultimate act of treason.

At one point, he was considered to be one of George Washington's rising stars.

His contributions during the Revolutionary War, specifically leading the troops at the Battles of Saratoga, were minimized and, to add salt to the wound, he never truly recovered from a freak accident that happened during the military action that unfolded September 19, 1777.

But who was Arnold as a person and why did he turn to the dark side?

The three-part television series *Washington,* which aired on the HISTORY Channel in February 2020, didn't shy away from controversies associated with the vilified public figure. The impressive crew of historians interviewed for the show, in fact, painted a somewhat sympathetic picture of the extremely complex man.

"Arnold was one of Washington's best officers," said Nathaniel Philbrick, author of *Bunker Hill.* "He was brilliant on the battlefield, decisive with a great strategic sense."

Edward G. Lengel agreed with Philbrick. "He was totally dedicated to the cause of the Revolution and he was willing to sacrifice for it," he said.

Arnold's daredevil approach ultimately resulted in an unprecedented win for the rebel troops. "Saratoga was a punch in the gut for the British army," Philbrick said. "They had assumed it would be victory and shut down the Revolution, but it was just the opposite."

But Arnold's heroics in Saratoga came at a price. In the final push of the battle, his left leg was shot and then crushed by his fallen horse. "He was taken to a hospital in Albany," explained author Alexis Coe.

"And, meanwhile, back in the center of the action was Horatio Gates who did not leave his tent during Saratoga but takes credit for Arnold's victory."

Gates was a British-born soldier who served as a leading American general during the early years of the American Revolution. In a coup to discredit and replace George Washington, Gates tried to claim responsibility for the win.

The truth eventually came out, but Arnold spent seven months recovering from the injury he incurred during the battle. Because of the wound, his left leg was two inches shorter than his right. Arnold, who donated his fortunes to the cause at the beginning of the war, met with Washington to ask for a raise.

"Washington clearly felt Arnold was worthy, but Congress decided not to give him the promotion," Philbrick said. "He was getting passed over by other people with political connections."

Coe said Arnold was struggling both physically and financially. "He's getting over his injury and Congress still hasn't repaid him what he fronted at the beginning of the war," she said. "He's in debt."

In June 1778, Arnold was offered a new opportunity to advance his career. The British had left Philadelphia to reinforce the troops in New York and Washington appointed Arnold as the military commander of the city.

"Washington saw Arnold as a kind of project," Philbrick explained. "Someone who could truly become a spectacular, balanced leader. Once in Philadelphia, Arnold thought it was time for him to profit from the war. He then launched into a series of investment schemes."

Arnold was accused of corruption but was eventually found innocent and basically was given a slap on the wrist for his actions. "He became, much in the way we saw a young Washington, embittered," Coe said. "But Washington didn't hold onto his past. Arnold tended to his grudges like a garden."

Soon after being court-martialed, Arnold started to sow the seeds of betrayal. He sent a letter to British Major John André, who was friends with Arnold's wife, Peggy Shippen, back when the British occupied Philadelphia.

By July 1779, Arnold was providing the enemy with military secrets as well as the locations of supply depots. While collecting compensation for the insider information, he eyed the massive fortification project known as West Point. "If the British capture West Point, they may be able to capture the entire Hudson River and decapitate the Revolution," explained Lengel.

By the time Washington agrees to the promotion, Arnold has been sharing secrets with the British for more than one year. He stands to earn thousands of pounds, a lifetime pension, and a British officer rank if he can deliver West Point, which he plans to do by sabotaging the fort's defenses from within.

As soon as Arnold is about to close the deal with the British, the plot is revealed. "André has made his way up the Hudson for a secret meeting with Arnold," Philbrick said. "On his way, André is captured by the militia. People begin to realize something is up."

Washington headed to Arnold's home as soon as he discovers the acts of treason, but he flees before the commander-in-chief arrives. Meanwhile, the letters he wrote started to surface and it's publicly revealed that he turned to the British and betrayed the nation.

Eventually escaping to New York City and ultimately New Brunswick in 1786, Arnold wasn't able to shake the negative stigma that followed him for the rest of his life. Struggling with a serious case of gout that first surfaced when he was injured in 1775, Arnold died on June 14, 1801. He was sixty years old.

ARNOLD'S HAUNT: INDEPENDENCE HALL

PHILADELPHIA, PA—The highlight of my trip to the "Birthplace of America" was actually walking inside Independence Hall and being able to soak in all of the history associated with the Georgian-style structure. Based on my visit, the building oozes three centuries of tumultuous history. It's an emotional tour de force.

After getting a comprehensive overview from the park rangers and seeing where the Continental Congress gathered to debate and approve the Declaration of Independence and ultimately the U.S. Constitution, I decided to take a ghost tour with a group that assembled in a garden outside of the Gilbert Stuart House, which was only one block away on Chestnut Street.

Yes, I wanted to get the scoop on Independence Hall's hauntings.

My tour guide, Kayla, was impressed I was able to go inside the historic structure. "Did they talk about the ghosts?" she asked. Nope. As someone who is extremely sensitive to the spirit realm, I told her it was overwhelming to visit a space with so much lingering energy.

It was so noticeable that I was surprised the park rangers didn't bring it up during their tour. "As a rule, rangers are told to say places in a state or national park are not haunted," Kayla explained. "But if you actually talk to them off the record, they will tell you that inexplicable things happen. But it's their official policy there are no ghosts."

Kayla told me it's fairly common for sensitives like myself to pick up on the "aura of disaster" imprinted in the walls of Independence Hall.

"Those who believe this place is haunted say there's a kaleidoscope of paranormal activity that has all sorts of ghosts, not necessarily because they died here, but because they're attracted to the energy of the building," she said. "There's a lot of competition for the spirits in Independence Hall and not enough energy to go around. So there are little things that happen all the time like doors opening and closing, books falling off of shelves, and sometimes furniture will move on its own."

Kayla said it's common for security guards to hear phantom footsteps inside the building. Also, they will often see a shadow figure on the second floor. "When the guards go to check it out, they don't see anything," she said, adding they often smell the strong smell of cigar smoke.

"Sometimes the footsteps will stop and then start up again," she said. "It's almost as if someone is waiting for you up on the second floor."

What's actually haunting Independence Hall? The tour guide believes the spirits are attracted to the energy and the symbolic significance of the building. "Even before it was Independence Hall, this was the Pennsylvania State House," she explained. "This is where the British controlled the colony of Pennsylvania and the city of Philadelphia. During the Revolutionary War, this was disputed territory."

For years, the British would bring their wounded troops to the building. If there was enough space, they would take them inside. If not, they would leave them in the yard outside of the building. "The idea was that a doctor would come and save the wounded troops, but there weren't enough doctors," she said. "Many of the soldiers died out here and in the hall. Maybe what haunts Independence Hall are some of the British troops that were left here to die and they were drawn in by the symbolic energy."

After the British fled Pennsylvania, Independence Hall was reclaimed. "It signified victory for the rebels," Kayla explained. "And that sense of victory continues to linger."

It's that symbolic duality that reportedly attracts famous spirits like Benjamin Franklin and Benedict Arnold, who was the military commander of Philadelphia during the transition in 1778. "Benedict Arnold died a bitter, remorseful man, who probably is restless and still trying to settle his troubles at Independence Hall," reported the website Haunt edHouses.com.

In addition to committing treason, Arnold was court-martialed and tried in Philadelphia. Even though he was cleared of the civil charges, Arnold's sour spirit supposedly paces back and forth through the hallowed rooms of Independence Hall replaying the event that eventually led to his downfall.

SPIRITS OF '76: SPIRITED DINING

It's so tragic. Living a life of fear and then reliving it for an eternity in the afterlife.

— Joni Mayhan, *Ghost Magnet*

The historic waterfront of Boston, Massachusetts, boasts a motley crew of nightlife locales rumored to be stomping grounds for spirits . . . and not the kind served in a chilled martini glass. In this section of *Ghosts of the American Revolution*, we feature two spirited dining locations including a centuries-old restaurant frequented by Daniel Webster and a local pub with a secret involving a horrific death caused by heavy machinery.

Apparently, the living aren't the only things that go bump in the nightlife.

Why haunted bars and restaurants? Joni Mayhan, author of *Dark and Scary Things,* told me spirits flock to familiar places. "Bars and restaurants are places where people feel comfortable. It's where they spend some of their happiest moments, which is why it makes sense they would also be haunted," Mayhan explained. "Spirits often return to the places where they remember happiness, hoping to reclaim some of the emotions they once felt."

Mayhan said the lingering energy at bars and restaurants serves as a "reservoir of energy" for ghosts. "Heightened emotions, such as joy and pleasure produce tremendous bursts of energy, something earthbound entities require," she said. "They will often flock to places where energy is prevalent in hopes of refueling themselves."

Why do ghosts stick around? Mayhan believes we're presented options at the time of death. "A white light might open up in front of us, or our late relatives and ancestors will come to help us," she explained. "Most people cross over immediately, not thinking twice about the process, but others balk. They might have loved ones they want to look out for or they might feel guilt over some grievance they experienced during their lifetime."

Mayhan suggested some choose to continue the party in the afterlife. "When souls remain earthbound, some of them wander around," she said. "They might visit their families, but they also find themselves drawn to places where they experienced pleasant memories. These places will include taverns, inns, and restaurants. In their view, they are still going out for an evening drink with friends."

Our first spirited dining stop is Union Oyster House near Faneuil Hall. History oozes from the wood-paneled walls of the oldest continuously operating restaurant in the United States, which originally opened in 1826. Before serving bivalves by the dozen and tall tumblers of brandy to nineteenth-century luminaries such as Senator Daniel Webster, who came to the restaurant's U-shaped mahogany oyster bar almost daily, it was an eighteenth-century dry-goods store and home to Isaiah Thomas's *Massachusetts Spy,* an anti-British tabloid that mobilized the rebellious Patriots in the years leading up to the Revolutionary War. Louis Philippe, former king of France, who was in exile after the revolution in his country, rented out the upstairs quarters in 1797, using the fake name of Duc de Chartres and giving French lessons to young women.

The Georgian-style structure located at 41–43 Union Street is so old that the original building, dating back to 1714 and erected a quarter of a century before Faneuil Hall, was waterfront property overlooking the Boston Harbor. Fishermen would maneuver their boats within a few feet of the oyster bar to deliver their catch of the day. America's first female server, Rose Carey, worked there in the early 1920s, and there's a photo of the waitress on the stairwell wall.

Owners of the restaurant introduced the toothpick to America in 1890, getting the idea from the natives in South America. President John F. Kennedy, when he was senator and congressman, would dine on the second floor of the Union Oyster House, reading the Sunday newspaper and eating lobster soup. There's a gold plaque bearing his likeness and honoring the former president at table eighteen, his favorite booth.

The structure was threatened in 1951 when a three-alarm fire swept through the second floor of the oyster house. Three firemen were injured, but the original raw bar and booths were unharmed. Some say the blaze stirred up spirits that had remained dormant for years.

In addition to its historical pedigree, which included kings, presidents, and even actors like Matt Damon and Meryl Streep, the Union Oyster House has long-standing reservations for a few of the building's resident spirits. There are far-fetched accounts of President Kennedy's ghost making a return visit to his Sunday haunt.

"The Kennedy family was known to be quite fond of the oyster house and JFK even has a booth dedicated to him," reported *Mental Floss,* adding that patrons claimed to have spotted "Kennedy's apparition wandering near his booth."

Also, many believe Daniel Webster, who notoriously devoured six plates of oysters while tossing back a tumbler of brandy almost daily, still holds court at the U-shaped oyster bar that bears his name. "Visitors to the Union Oyster House come not so much for the food as for the thrill of eating the same dish in the same spot as some of America's historical figures," reported an online restaurant site called Eater, alluding to former presidents like Calvin Coolidge, Franklin D. Roosevelt, and William Clinton, who dined there when they visited Boston. "You can claim a stool at the raw bar and slurp oysters next to the ghost of Senator Daniel Webster, a regular who daily enjoyed his tumblers of brandy with oysters on the half shell." For the record, Webster became a Massachusetts senator in 1827, one year after the restaurant opened as the Atwood & Bacon Oyster House.

Bob Eshback, a veteran shucker and bartender at Webster's namesake hangout, told me he and other employees have experienced paranormal activity in the Union Oyster House's basement. Contrary to the ghostly rumors, the late nineteenth-century senator reportedly left the building years ago, and JFK hasn't made a post-mortem comeback. When asked where Webster sat in the 1800s, Eshback said it was standing room only for the restaurant's most revered patron. "He didn't sit, he stood," Eshback responded. "There were no stools back then."

While Eshback claimed to be more of a skeptic than a believer, he said he felt "a presence" or an odd energy emanating from the downstairs area when he started working for the restaurant in 1999. "There are reports of a busboy or a dishwasher committing suicide in the basement in the early twentieth century or possibly the late nineteenth century," Eshback explained, adding that he hasn't felt the ghostly energy recently, but he avoided the storage area below when he first tended bar in the late 1990s. "Many people who have worked here didn't like going down there because of the presence."

A short walk from Boston's Union Oyster House is Ned Devine's, which is also rumored to be haunted. Originally built in 1742, the hallowed halls of Faneuil Hall have seen its share of Boston history, including the early meetings to plan the "tea action," better known as the Boston Tea Party, and the establishment of the Committee of Correspondence. The structure's gilded grasshopper weathervane, made out of copper and believed to be modeled after a similar design for the London Royal Exchange, includes a time capsule from Boston's past and boasts old coins, newspaper clippings, and secret messages from former mayors.

Faneuil Hall was waterfront property until the 1800s when Bostonians filled in the harbor in a process known as "wharfing out." The landmark was expanded in 1826 to include Quincy Market. The first open-air market in the country is now home to many shops, restaurants, push carts, and street performers.

Ned Devine's, a popular Irish pub and restaurant in Faneuil Hall's Quincy Market, faces Boston Harbor and is believed to entertain a ghost or two. "Considering the bar's location in the historic Quincy Market and the history that goes along with that, it's no surprise," reported the website BostInno in 2014. "According to Ned's staff, they've had everything from moving salt and pepper shakers on tables to sightings of ghost-like images in the club and basement. An apparition rolling a barrel down the hall has also been seen haunting the bar."

The *Boston Globe* confirmed the rumors in 2015. "In Boston, you've got to have at least one haunted Irish bar. Ned Devine's in Faneuil Hall is the chosen one," reported the *Globe*. A restaurant spokesperson said, "Some of the staff and management have claimed to hear voices and see a colonial woman spirit at night."

After spending several spirited lunches at the alleged haunt, I heard stories of a woman wearing period garb in the pub's dancefloor area and one waitress swore she heard horrific screams—as if someone was in extreme pain—in the bar's club area. Why would staffers report these tortuous cries from beyond?

After doing some research, I learned that Ned Devine's is in the spot formerly occupied by Ames Plow Company, which sold tractors and farming equipment. "From 1862 to 1909 the rooms in the wings of Quincy Hall were devoted to the sale of agricultural implements by the Ames Plow Company," reported the City of Boston's landmark commission report in 1975. "In 1913, this upper level was subdivided into twenty-two offices by the Ames Plow Company. The attic space held lockers that were rented out by the market's grocers and butchers."

A source who wished to remain anonymous told *Ghosts of the American Revolution* that the screams may somehow be related to its Ames Plow past. "Someone probably got caught in the equipment and was screaming," he continued.

Based on a horrific death in 1907, the theory may be a viable explanation for the screams of pain heard by Ned Devine's staff. According to a police report from September 19, Victor Hendrickson from Worcester died instantly while messing with the agricultural equipment at Faneuil Hall's Ames Plow Company. "Hendrickson was adjusting a nut on a stay rod, working on a ladder, with another person holding the ladder at the bottom. In some way, his coat caught the coupling on the shaft of his right side, throwing him around the shaft," Boston's police chief reported in 1907. "He was killed instantly. His body swung around on the coupling until the power was stopped. The shafting was fourteen inches distant from the ladder on which he was working."

Based on the research of famed paranormal investigators like the late, great Dr. Hans Holzer, it's common for spirits who have died accidentally to stick around. Some believe the ghost at Ned Devine's may be what is known as a "stay behind."

Holzer, in an interview in 2005, explained the phenomenon. "'Stay behinds' are relatively common," he said. "Somebody dies, and then they're really surprised that all of a sudden they're not dead. They're alive like they were. They don't understand it because they weren't prepared for it. So they go back to what they knew most—their chair, their room, and they just sit there. Next, they want to let people know that they're still 'alive.' So they'll do little things like moving things, appearing to relatives, pushing objects, poltergeist phenomena, and so on."

Reports of a barrel mysteriously rolling in Ned Devine's bar area and the inexplicable moving of salt-and-pepper shakers at the restaurant is typical poltergeist behavior and is generally attributed to so-called "stay behind" ghosts.

What about the woman wearing period garb who's also been spotted by Ned Devine's staffers? The history pre-dating Faneuil Hall needed to be explored to uncover the backstory of the ghostly woman. "The Hall was built on top of a landfill that covers what used to be the old Town Dock, which served as Boston's port, center of commerce and city meeting place in the seventeenth and eighteenth centuries," reported the *Archaeology News Network*.

Sean Hennessey, a spokesperson with the National Park Service, said the area also has a dark history that is often overlooked. "Colonists held slave auctions right next to where Faneuil Hall was built," Hennessey explained. "Ironically, Peter Faneuil, the wealthy merchant and benefactor of Faneuil Hall, was involved in the slave trade. The 'Cradle of Liberty,' as the Hall is often called due to the revolutionary activities that took place there, was actually built from funds derived from the slave trade."

Author Joni Mayhan said the male energy at the restaurant could have ties to Faneuil's human-trafficking past. "If he was a slave trader, he might feel a sense of guilt for what he did," she told me. "Religion teaches us that bad people go to hell, so it's possible he's worried about the ramifications of crossing over. Or he could just be an angry bastard who wants to hang around so he can wreak more havoc on the living."

For the record, the colonists imported slaves from West Africa to the West Indies in 1644, but it wasn't until 1676 that the African-trade operation was considered successful. By 1676, Boston ships pioneered a slave trade to Madagascar and then inhumanely sold human cargo to Virginians in 1678. If they couldn't sell these human beings due to illness or gender, the Puritans brought the undesirables back to New England and they were allocated to local families. In fact, famed poet and enslaved woman Phillis Wheatley came to Boston and was most likely sold in the former Town Dock area near present-day Faneuil Hall.

So, what about the girl ghost? Perhaps the female spirit spotted by staffers at Ned Devine's is also related to Boston's sadistic past. According to reports, the full-bodied apparition of the woman seen peeking around the corners of the two-floor restaurant looks terrified.

Mayhan said the horrors of Boston's slave trade may have carried over into the afterlife. "If the traders still have control of them, they might have forced them to stay," Mayhan told me, adding that the theory saddens her but she's seen evidence of it at other haunted locations with a history of slavery. "It's so tragic. Living a life of fear and then reliving it for an eternity in the afterlife."

JOHN BURGOYNE

British General John Burgoyne was seriously shocked when he lost the Battle of Saratoga in 1777. The campaign included two military engagements—fought eighteen days apart—and was considered to be a crucial win and a major turning point for the Continental Army during the American Revolution.

Burgoyne's response to the defeat in Saratoga, New York, was dramatic. "There was a wonderful letter from a British officer that described how Burgoyne was so full of emotion and disbelief that he really couldn't speak," said Joanne B. Freeman on the HISTORY Channel documentary called *Washington*.

Gentleman Johnny, as he was nicknamed by his aristocratic friends when he was younger, had high expectations. In hindsight, his optimism may have been unrealistic. After capturing Fort Ticonderoga and Fort Edward, he didn't have the support needed from his fellow British commanders. He also expected the American Loyalists would join the campaign as he moved south through New York, but they didn't.

On October 17, 1777, Burgoyne begrudgingly raised the white flag.

Instead of an unconditional surrender, Burgoyne rallied for what was called a "Convention Army," which involved his men handing over their weapons and returning to Europe with a promise never to return to the region. The general's troops, estimated to be under six thousand, were marched from New York to Cambridge, Massachusetts. They arrived on November 8, 1777, after hiking for weeks and were held in crude barracks left over from the Siege of Boston.

Meanwhile, no one in Cambridge wanted to take Burgoyne in as a boarder, so he was forced to set up his quarters at the Blue Anchor Tavern, a popular gathering spot near Winthrop Park in Harvard Square, before convincing leaders to move him into the more plush Apthorp

House. They granted the general his wish, but he was forced to buy his own furniture and pay rent.

The Continental Congress rejected the treaty after deliberating over the terms of the British surrender and Burgoyne was shipped back to England. His remaining troops—which included British, Canadian, and German Hessian soldiers—were incarcerated in inhumane prisons scattered throughout Massachusetts and Virginia.

Conditions were harsh and historians view the severity of the retaliatory response as revenge for the treatment of Continental Army prisoners on ships like the *Jersey* off the coast of modern-day Brooklyn Navy Yard.

Burgoyne faced heavy criticism when he returned to London. He was unable to clear his name and then spent one year as the commander-in-chief of Ireland before completely retiring from the military.

Gentleman Johnny has been lampooned by history. He's often presented as a British aristocrat who became a military leader, not by ability, but because of his political connections. Historians like George Billias, who characterized Burgoyne as "a buffoon in uniform who bungled his assignments badly" in the book *George Washington's Opponents*, continue to criticize him.

While hashing out military strategy wasn't his cup of tea, the fallen general did have a flair for theatrics. He wrote two plays including *Maid of the Oaks* and his well-respected *The Heiress* in 1786. Burgoyne died on August 4, 1792, and was buried in London's Westminster Abbey. He was seventy years old.

BURGOYNE'S HAUNT: APTHORP HOUSE

CAMBRIDGE, MA—Built in 1760, the clapboard Apthorp House—which predates the rest of Harvard's houses by several decades—is the main residence of Harvard's Adams House master, or a senior faculty member who presides over the upper-class dormitory. According to campus ghost lore, it's also home to the ghosts of Revolutionary War soldiers, among them British general John Burgoyne, who was imprisoned there during the war. Legend has it Burgoyne's ghost still haunts the structure.

Apthorp House was one of the largest and most distinguished colonial residences in early Cambridge, surrounded by grounds that originally extended toward the Charles River. President and Harvard alum John Adams wrote, "A great house, at that time thought to be a splendid palace, was built by Mr. Apthorp at Cambridge." Its grandeur aroused suspicions among Cambridge's gossip mongers, who claimed Christ Church's Reverend East Apthorp harbored a secret passion to become a bishop. The son of a British-born merchant, Apthorp fled to Britain in 1764 to avoid ridicule from the city's venom-spewing Congregationalists, who labeled his home "the Bishop's Palace."

After Apthorp escaped, John Borland purchased the house and added a third floor. However, his Tory leanings didn't sit well with the anti-Loyalist movement in the days leading up to the Revolutionary War in Cambridge, and he left the house in 1775.

Burgoyne, who retreated with troops after losing the Battle of Saratoga in 1777, was held prisoner in the estate and apparently had issues with the property. His dislike for the less-than-stellar living arrangements reportedly carried over to the afterlife. "Legend has it that Burgoyne's ghost still haunts the house," confirmed the Adams House website. "Like many subsequent tenants in Cambridge, he complained bitterly about the lack of furnishings and the exorbitant rent he was forced to pay."

Harvard's *Crimson* newspaper, whose office is located directly across the street from Apthorp, alluded to the "fearsome phantoms" lurking in the 250-year-old house. "I hear them rumbling about all the time," said Hannah L. Bouldin, who lived in the attic in the 1980s and claimed Apthorp's soldier spirits helped her finish her exam. Jana M. Kiely, a former co-master at Adams, added fire to the Burgoyne myth. "General Burgoyne is still complaining about the high rent of Harvard property and wants the university to do something about it," Kiely joked.

Matthew Swayne, author of *America's Haunted Universities*, suggested Burgoyne's ghost is possibly a residual apparition. "Burgoyne's anger and frustration must have imprinted itself on the psychic fiber of Apthorp," he wrote.

Apthorp House, which is surrounded by three "Gold Coast" dormitories that were built around 1900 to offer luxury accommodations for

Harvard's elite, is literally in the center of what is possibly the college's most haunted corridor. "One house in particular—Adams House—is rumored to have the most ghosts," claimed Swayne in his book. Franklin D. Roosevelt, who lived in Westmorly Court (now B-17) from 1900 to 1904, was a famous Adams House alum. Oddly, there's a mysterious death associated with Roosevelt's distant relative Stewart Douglas Robinson, who tragically fell from his room at Hampden Hall, which is currently home to the Harvard Book Store.

To add some "boo" to the house's ghost lore, a novel written in 2000 by alum Sean Desmond called *Adams Fall* talked about the dorm's "severe Gothic quality." In fact, the murder mystery used the house as a metaphor for the protagonist's mental demise and described, in detail, the spook factor surrounding the "stone monster" structure. "A resident of Adams house's reportedly haunted B-entry, he's familiar with tales of phantom footsteps, vanished laundry, lurking shadows," Desmond wrote. "But when he begins to find himself the object of the house's cruel attentions, his world quickly begins to unravel." In one scene, Desmond's protagonist asked if Adams's B-entry was, in fact, haunted. "I know it is," responded a fictional female student. "It feels damned. . . . The pipes make these weird noises. And sometimes there's the smell in the hallway and closets."

Oddly, there's a cryptic message circulating online alluding to the spirits of Adams House. "There's a ghost who lives underneath the dining hall in a crawl space," wrote an anonymous source. "If you have a tutor let you into the steam vents, you can hear her cry."

SALLY HUTCHINSON

Sarah Hutchinson Oliver, nicknamed "Sally" by her family, was the daughter of the British governor of Massachusetts Bay who was later chased out of her home in 1775. In the years leading up to the American Revolution, the Loyalist woman's livelihood was destroyed. Sadly, she was no stranger to tragedy.

A few days after she was proposed to by Peter Oliver, Hutchinson was caught in the middle of the growing tensions once the Stamp Act was passed. In August 1765, the Sons of Liberty organized a protest to hang and burn her fiancé's uncle in effigy. The mob marched to Andrew Oliver's house and threatened to destroy it unless he quit his job as a stamp agent. Oliver resigned immediately.

The crowd, still out for blood, besieged the lieutenant governor's house and directed their wrath toward Sally's father, demanding a public denouncement of the Stamp Act. Thomas Hutchinson was able to avoid the conflict at first, but the mob returned on August 26, 1765, and approached the family's home in the North End.

The protestors stormed the house and Sally found refuge with a neighbor. Her father, however, stayed behind to face the angry mob. Concerned he would be murdered, Sally begged him to leave. While she was in the house, the group surrounded the property and the father and daughter were barely able to escape. The Hutchinsons ended up spending the night with their relative, Samuel Mather.

Christy Parrish, manager of the Oliver House, said the mob scene was just the beginning of Sally's downward spiral. "When she and Peter were married in February 1770, this home was a wedding gift from Judge Oliver," Parrish said. "For the first time in her life, she could express her style and have a say in how the house was run. She was and continues to be the first lady of the house."

Things quickly changed for Mrs. Peter Oliver. She became pregnant with her first child, Margaret Hutchinson Oliver, and the newborn was delivered in 1771. "The baby was born small, weak, and was struggling to survive," Parrish explained. "For five months, Sally nurtured her first born, never wavering in her attempt to help the baby. Her husband wrote of her love and dedication in his journal. Despite her efforts the baby just wasn't able to continue to breathe."

Parrish said Sally was likely suffering from postpartum depression coupled with the grief associated with losing her daughter. "She went through a very difficult grieving process, and most likely continued to feel this void for the remainder of her life," she said. "One can't help but wonder if baby Margaret was buried on the property, though we haven't discovered a grave yet, the property is thick with brush and trees so it's highly possible that someday we will find her."

The manager of the Oliver House believes spirits continue to linger at a location because of unfinished business or, perhaps, the property was seen as a safe haven when they were alive. "It's definitely possible that Sally wanders the house because of both of these reasons," Parrish told me. "I believe her spirit has been reunited with her baby and remains in the house that she had such a major role in creating."

Sally and her family fled to Boston in 1775 because their home was confiscated by the Sons of Liberty. The Oliver House historian believes Hutchinson is reclaiming what she loved the most. "She craved to return to the small house where she felt more responsibility than any other time in her life," Parrish said. "She didn't have a voice in 1775 when they con-fiscated her home and belongings. She certainly has a say in the afterlife."

Sally Hutchinson Oliver became ill after giving birth to a son in the winter of 1780. Her father, Thomas, died a few months later after being exiled in London and, after a great deal of misery and distress, Sally passed from complications associated with childbirth on June 28, 1780. She was only thirty-five years old.

HUTCHINSON'S HAUNT: OLIVER HOUSE

MIDDLEBORO, MA—Within a few moments after visiting the Oliver House during the research phase of *Ghosts of the American Revolution*, I clearly heard a female say, "Help me." She was desperate and her tortured words seemed like they were directed at me. A few minutes after hearing the disembodied voice, a bannister from the stairwell mysteriously popped out and fell to the ground.

I asked the manager of the Oliver House, Christy Parrish, about the female voice and she said I was connecting with Bethania Sproat, daughter of Thomas Weston. Over a three-year period in the 1840s, Sproat and her husband Earle tragically lost three of their children. She suffered a miscarriage in 1841 and their toddler daughter Abby was killed after a kettle of boiling water fell on her, fatally scalding the child. Her son James died from pneumonia in 1844 and, twenty years later in 1864, Sproat's husband was stricken with tuberculosis.

Yes, the woman's life was marred by tragedy.

When I walked upstairs to the second-floor bedroom closet to put on a Revolutionary War–era jacket for a photo shoot, I clearly heard another female voice express a similar sentiment, but her comments were more about being trapped in the house. According to the volunteers at the Oliver House, I was connecting with Julie, a Revolutionary War–era chambermaid.

With that said, I'm haunted by those voices. If I have a soft spot when it comes to the spirit realm it's specifically those who have been oppressed when they were alive. I pray the trauma doesn't continue in the afterlife.

How can I help them? I'm a believer that if I tell their story and sort through their unfinished business, I can somehow give the spirits closure. When it comes to the lingering energy associated with Sally Hutchinson Oliver, however, there wasn't a clear-cut solution to ease her pain in the afterlife.

Like Sproat, Hutchinson lost everything she loved including her first-born child. In 1775, she lost her house and then her father and her life in 1780.

"There was a lot of loss at the house. There was loss of life, safety, and ownership," Parrish told me. "When a person is essentially stripped of everything, then sadness will prevail. The energies that reside inside the house run the gamut. There's loneliness, particularly with Sally's spirit.

She endured so much during her brief time there. Her father fled Boston and travelled to England in 1774, so he died before she was able to see him again."

Mrs. Peter Oliver was also dealing with financial insecurity. "Peter had been forced to sign documents that he would not accept money from General Gage, so she had now lost the means to pay for things they needed," Parrish explained. "Peter was not allowed to practice medicine. She experienced the suffocation from the Sons of Liberty who were systematically forcing her family to a breaking point."

As I toured the Oliver House, I kept picking up on severe depression. I was told by the Oliver House's manager that she also empathically feels Hutchinson's pain. "She had endured so much stress that this was causing her a terrible amount of depression," Parrish said. "They were alone and defenseless. There was always the fear she would get the word her father or siblings had been killed. It's that constant day-to-day anxiety and sadness that has been psychically imprinted on the home."

Is the Oliver House cursed? Chris Andrade, a volunteer and paranormal investigator, said the fatal injuries that occurred on the property likely could have been treated with modern medicine. "Unfortunately, the Olivers were victims of their own circumstance and time," Andrade told me. "If Sally had given birth today, her baby girl Margaret probably would have survived and I feel the same about Bethania's child. I believe Abby would have likely survived her burns with proper medical treatment."

Andrade continued: "I can understand why the Oliver House would almost seem cursed, but it's not."

THOMAS GAGE

General Thomas Gage made one major mistake when he assumed the position as the Massachusetts Bay Colony's military governor in 1774. He underestimated the underdog.

In 1763, Gage was appointed as the commander-in-chief of the British forces in North America, which was the highest-ranking post in the colonies. In the role, he imposed retaliatory actions against the colonists. For example, he convinced Parliament to close the harbor in response to the Boston Tea Party, forcing merchants to pay for the damages.

When he replaced Thomas Hutchinson as Massachusetts's military governor during the onset of the American Revolution, he ordered the redcoats to march toward Concord and Lexington in an attempt to find hidden ammunition and capture the notorious troublemaker, Samuel Adams. Of course, Adams managed to escape. But the presence of the British regulars resulted in the pivotal first battle that ultimately kicked off the War of Independence.

"The chaotic skirmishing at Lexington and Concord in April 1775 left the British holed up in Boston and hostile colonists occupying the city's surrounds," wrote Tony Horwitz in the May 2013 edition of *Smithsonian* magazine. "But it remained unclear whether the ill-equipped rebels were willing or able to engage the British Army in pitched battle. Leaders on both sides also thought the conflict might yet be settled without full-scale war."

Gage was caught off guard but convinced his well-trained British officers could contain the Patriot fighters gathered in Cambridge, Massachusetts. He was wrong. Gage's greatest miscalculation unfolded on June 17, 1775, on Breed's Hill in Charlestown.

"When the rebels opened fire, the close-packed British fell in clumps. In some spots, the British lines became jumbled, making them even easier targets," Horwitz reported. "The Americans added to the chaos by aiming at officers, distinguished by their fine uniforms. The attackers, repulsed at every point, were forced to withdraw."

The British were hit hard with 1,054 regulars killed or wounded. The Americans had around 400 soldiers down with 115 fatalities. The first true military engagement of the Revolutionary War was considered a Pyrrhic victory in that it inflicted such a devastating toll on the winner that it's basically considered a defeat.

The Battle of Bunker Hill proved to be the military governor's greatest downfall. In a letter to Great Britain's secretary of war, Gage characterized the Patriots as "spirited up by rage and enthusiasm" and finally realized the rebel fighters were passionate about the cause. "These people show a spirit and conduct against us they never showed against the French," he wrote. "The loss we have sustained is greater than we can bear. Small armies cannot afford such losses, especially when the advantage gained tends to do little more than the gaining of a post."

Three days after authorities received Gage's report from across the pond, he was replaced by General William Howe. The British leader received the order in September and returned to England on October 11, 1775. He returned to his posh family home in London's Portland Place.

As the flames of the Revolutionary War engulfed North America, he attempted to help the displaced Loyalists recover the losses they incurred after fleeing the colonies. Gage also received visitors to his palatial estate including the man he replaced as governor, Thomas Hutchinson, who was chased out of his home by the Sons of Liberty.

Gage died in London's Portland Place on April 2, 1787. He was in his late sixties.

GAGE'S HAUNT: OLD POWDER HOUSE

SOMERVILLE, MA—The ominous stone tower overlooking the six-way intersection at Somerville's Nathan Tufts Park was initially built as a windmill by John Mallet in 1703 and then transformed into a powder magazine. In 1774, the British military governor, Thomas Gage, confiscated the 250 barrels of gunpowder stored in the round structure so the ammunition wouldn't be used by the American Patriots during the Revolutionary War. Musket-toting colonists—ticked off by Gage's orders to steal the powder—made their way to Cambridge, ready to fight. It's estimated fifty thousand armed men from across the colonies responded to the word-of-mouth alarm.

Resting on a hill close to Tufts University, the Old Powder House has a colorful and allegedly haunted history that can be traced back to before the war. Included in this backstory are sightings of a cranky old spirit who haunts the mill on windy nights and spews curse words at passersby. In addition to the foul-mouthed apparition, reports suggest some kind of residual energy of past trauma exists in the form of a phantom ball of blue sparks.

Why is the ghost so angry? According to Charles Skinner in *Myths and Legends of Our Own Land,* the old mill was the site of a tragic love story. Apparently, a penniless Somerville farmer and his girlfriend, the daughter of a wealthy landowner, once used the stone structure as a regular meeting place. One night, the father followed his daughter to her secret love nest. The maiden hid at the top of the mill to avoid her pops. She grabbed a rope to shimmy up the structure and somehow managed to set off the windmill's machinery. Her father's arm was accidentally severed by the grinding millstone. The girl's lover arrived, and they carried her father home. The father's injuries were fatal. However, his spirit is rumored to live on at the Old Powder House.

"Before she could summon her heart to fix the wedding day, the girl passed many months of grief and repentance, and for the rest of her life, she avoided the old mill," wrote Skinner. "There was good reason for doing so, people said, for on windy nights, the spirits of the old man used to haunt the place, using such profanity that it became visible in the form of blue lights, dancing and exploding about the building."

Yep, the old man's ghost was cussing up a blue streak. There's also a contemporary retelling of the ghost story that involved a cross-dressing woman. "One version of the story tells of a young woman, dressed as a man, who sought refuge in the loft one night. But somehow a man who was up to no good discovered she was actually a woman and tried to molest her," explained Cheri Revai in *Haunted Massachusetts.* "In the process, he became entangled in the mill's machinery and died. His restless spirit is said to still haunt the Powder House today."

Incidentally, the spirit's potty-mouthed antics continue to live on with hot headed drivers and pedestrians trying to navigate the six-lane rotary in front of the haunted sentinel. In fact, Powderhouse Circle has the claim to fame of having the most motor-vehicle collisions in Somerville based on statistics collected by the city's SomerStat group. Massachusetts drivers? Now that's scary.

HESSIAN SPIRITS OF '76

On a cold November morning in 1776, a mounted Hessian soldier was decapitated by a cannonball at that spot.
—Christopher Rondina, *Legends of Sleepy Hollow*

British invasion? Not exactly. The residual redcoats spotted throughout New England may be hired killers known as Hessians. The German mercenaries served among the English forces during the American Revolution and, in several cases, their spirits continue to linger in the afterlife.

The Hessian soldiers were strangers in a foreign land. Many of them died very tragic deaths, fighting in bloody battles with minimal pay or motivation. Because of their lack of passion for the war they were fighting, would this result in a potential haunting?

Christopher Rondina, a paranormal-themed author and tour guide based in Newport, Rhode Island, thinks it's a viable possibility. He strongly believes they were victims of false promises and suggested a few of the Hessians are sticking around in search of postmortem justice.

"Many of the Hessian soldiers came here having been promised land in this new, wide-open nation," Rondina told me, "Since so many Hessians had little chance of bettering their situation in the princedoms of feudal Germany, they pinned their dreams here in the New World. They essentially bet everything on a hollow promise that would never be fulfilled. Many of them died knowing they traveled halfway across the world for nothing."

Rondina noted the Hessians saw little-to-no money for their services because the British made a deal with the princes who ruled their homeland. "The soldiers received their standard pay, if any, plus food, gear, and little else," he said.

It's also important to note that those who survived the Revolutionary War did end up staying in America. Many of the Hessians were able to assimilate into the German communities that were already settled in Pennsylvania, New York, and New Jersey.

The casualties, however, weren't so lucky.

One of the more well-known Hessian ghosts has been turning heads for two centuries. In *Legends of Sleepy Hollow: The Lost*

History of the Headless Horseman, Rondina explored the real-life inspiration behind many of the characters featured in Washington Irving's classic, including the ghostly antagonist believed to be a Revolutionary War–era Hessian soldier.

"I learned some fascinating and unexpected facts while researching the story, including a real Ichabod Crane who had served in the military with Washington Irving," he told me. "He wasn't pleased at all with his inclusion in the story."

Rondina's most extraordinary discovery, however, was that a genuine Revolutionary War soldier had been the inspiration for the Headless Horseman legend.

"He was alleged to be a German mercenary working for the British Army, but his identity was unknown, even 200 years later," he said. "I believed the answer to his mystery had to be out there somewhere, so I began digging, looking for any clues to the ghost's mortal existence. The answer was out there, but I had to go to Germany to find it, hidden among centuries-old military records."

Based on his research, Rondina said a real-life tragedy at the Battlefield at Merritt Hill in White Plains inspired Irving. "On a cold November morning in 1776, a mounted Hessian soldier was decapitated by a cannonball at that spot, just as Washington Irving's story says," Rondina confirmed. "The site today is rural and quiet, but the wooded hillside gives off an eerie energy that can't be denied. It's the very site where the Hessian restlessly searches each night for his long-lost head."

In addition to the ghost associated with Irving's "The Legend of Sleepy Hollow," there's a supposed Hessian-related haunting in Cambridge, Massachusetts.

Built in 1685 by Dr. Richard Hooper as a typical "first-period" farmhouse, the Hooper-Lee-Nichols House has seen its share of tragedy. "Some very grim things happened here," said Gavin W. Kleespies, the former executive director of the Cambridge Historical Society. "All of these houses on Tory Row are extremely old, and very bad things happened in all of them. As far as this house, it's pushing 330 years, and lots of people have died here," he said as he gave a spirited tour of the second-oldest house in Cambridge in 2013. "Is it haunted? I don't know."

Kleespies, whose former office was based in the historic Tory Row home, has an encyclopedic knowledge of the structure's tumultuous history. As far as ghost lore, however, he's quick to shoot down a rumor that has snowballed since the 1980s. According to an article in the *Harvard Crimson* from October 31, 1986, "The Hooper-Lee-Nichols House on Brattle Street is said to be home to the ghosts of five Hessian mercenaries who fought in the Revolution. Legend has it they first appeared in 1915, when a library was built on the site of their graves. The Hessian quintet has been playing cards in the room ever since."

Fact? Kleespies said the Hessian legend is probably not historically accurate. "There's not a lot of truth to that story," he remarked. "There have been excavations to this site, and there are all sorts of myths that have been debunked. For example, people said the house was a stop on the Underground Railroad. However, there's no evidence to support that claim."

The historian did point out a three-year period, from 1774 to 1777, when the house was vacated by noted British Loyalist judge Joseph Lee, who fled Tory Row days after the Powder Alarm, a precursor to the Revolution, when thousands of angry Patriots from surrounding towns prepared to march toward Boston for battle. However, Lee got out before the tumult. It seems the September 1, 1774, alarm was a bit premature.

"Lee actually moved back in 1777 to reclaim his property, and unlike many of the houses in the area that were turned into quarters for the Convention Troops, his house was spared," Kleespies said, adding that it's unlikely the German mercenaries were buried on the property.

Kleespies, however, said there's no concrete proof to contradict the claim. "It's possible because there were many officers who needed places to stay. But it was never recorded that Hessian soldiers actually stayed here," he said. "I mean, they could have stayed somewhere on Joseph Lee's property, but it's highly unlikely. The property was forty-five acres at the time, so it's inevitable that soldiers camped out somewhere near the house."

While Kleespies is quick to debunk the Hessian soldier myth, he does point out the macabre periods in the house's early years, especially after its original owner, Dr. Richard Hooper, died in 1691. "As far as the house being haunted, the American Revolution may be flashy, but the original owners have a very dark story," Kleespies said. Hooper's wife, Elizabeth, took in boarders, and the property then began to fall into disrepair until her mysterious death in 1701.

"When Hooper died, he left a formidable estate. Within one year of his death, Hooper's wife fell on bad times and petitioned to be able to serve liquor. This is the 1690s, and by the time she passes, this house is just devastated. It's completely trashed," Kleespies said, adding that her dead body was found wrapped in a sheet. "There's a whole mystery about the house from 1701 to 1716. We don't know what happened. Are there any ghosts in the house from that period? Not sure. I wouldn't say it was a house of ill repute, but it was definitely a house no one wanted to be associated with for fifteen years."

Fast-forward to the mid-nineteenth century, when the Nichols family moved into the Brattle Street estate. In 1850, George and Susan Nichols rented and began to renovate the house, installing a roof balustrade that was once part of Boston's St. Paul's Cathedral. One of the Nichols children married a Civil War officer, and her young daughter died tragically in the house. "It was the Fourth of July, and her daughter stepped on fireworks, got an infection and died," Kleespies said. "The Nichols daughter was devastated."

As far as residual energy lingering in the Hooper-Lee-Nichols House, Kleespies said he was convinced for years that the seventeenth-century structure was indeed haunted. In fact, Kleespies said he had a few close encounters in the early 1990s. "I don't know if it was because I was a lot younger and impressionable, but if you asked me back then I would have said, without hesitation, this place is definitely haunted," he said. "Creepy stuff happened. Doors opened and closed. Objects would mysteriously move to different locations. If you were here by yourself, you would hear noises."

Kleespies, who moved to Chicago to work on his master's degree, returned to the Hooper-Lee-Nichols House in 2008. During his stint with the Cambridge Historical Society, he didn't encounter anything paranormal. "I'm here all the time—I'm even here Halloween at night—and nothing seems to bother me," he told me in an interview in 2013. "Maybe the house is happier? It's hard to say."

However, the Hooper-Lee-Nichols's former resident fellows, who slept near the Cambridge Historical Society's archive, have approached Kleespies with creepy tales involving ghostly encounters. Kleespies's theory? Perhaps the spirits are attracted to the library's archives.

"One of our resident fellows would swear to this day that this house is haunted," Kleespies told me. "Maybe it's the archives that are haunted? I don't know. We have a lot of stuff that meant a lot to many people who are no longer with us, like locks of hair, and if this place is haunted, it would be the archives. Maybe that's what's so scary."

While historians can't prove Hessians were imprisoned at the Hooper-Lee-Nichols House, it's a fact that thousands were kept in less-than-ideal holding barracks with only two floors and twenty-four rooms in Rutland, Massachusetts.

Joni Mayhan, author of two dozen paranormal-themed books, believes there is an indelible scar imprinted on the land near the Quabbin Reservoir. "I've been to the location where the barracks once stood. The land is now personal property, but I didn't need to walk onto the property to feel the overwhelming emotion of sadness and despondency that lingered there," Mayhan told me.

When General John Burgoyne was forced to surrender his entire army of six thousand Hessian soldiers in late 1777 after losing the Battle of Saratoga, the tiny Central Massachusetts hamlet hosted many of the colonial militia's prisoners of war. Rutland's tiny population swelled dramatically. In fact, at least three thousand soldiers were crammed into the makeshift prison.

"The Hessians weren't treated well," Mayhan said. "They were overcrowded, didn't have enough food, and no heat. This wasn't even their battle, but they were being punished for their participation."

Mayhan said it's important to view the Hessian soldiers as human beings. "We like to think of them as the enemy, but they were living, breathing people as well," she said. "They were forced to endure horrific conditions and many of them died far from home. That kind of trauma leaves an imprint on the land, something people will feel for centuries."

The structure used to incarcerate the Hessians was razed in the late 1880s. In 1903, the state built an equally inhumane prison camp less than a mile from the Revolutionary War–era holding barracks. Mayhan said the land is teeming with spirits.

"I spent an entire summer exploring the grounds and conducting paranormal research at the Rutland Prison Camp ruins," she said. "The area was haunted, which was evident by the plethora of EVPs we were getting on our digital recorders. What I didn't realize was there was a very negative entity there that would follow me home and make my life a living hell."

Mayhan documented her terrifying experience with the attachment in her book, *Soul Collector*.

"I believe the negative energy the Hessian soldiers left behind permeated the entire area, changing the energetic composition," she said. "What started out as a peaceful plot of land with beautiful views and meandering streams quickly turned into a literal cesspool of dark energy."

TOWN CRIER Q&A: RICHARD ESTEP

*Those Brits who died far from home may well be trapped, unsure
of how to move on.*
—Richard Estep, *Paranormal Night Shift*

Richard Estep, author of *The Farnsworth House Haunting* and the
featured expert on television shows like *Paranormal Night Shift*
and *Haunted Hospitals*, told me his fellow British friends who live
across the pond aren't that interested in the American Revolution.
Why? "Possibly because it was one of our military defeats," he
said wryly.

When it comes to historical interests, Estep isn't a typical
Brit. "I've always been an enthusiast of the Civil War in the United
States ever since I was a boy. Learning about a conflict just a
century beforehand fought with similar tactics but slightly more
outmoded weaponry fascinated me."

Originally from England's Leicester, Estep moved to Colorado
as an adult and investigated haunted locations for years before
writing his first memoir, *In Search of the Paranormal*, in 2015. In
fact, he spent a week in the haunted Fort Mifflin, one of the only
intact Revolutionary War battlefields and the only fortification in
Philadelphia, Pennsylvania.

Photo courtesy Richard Estep

Is it important to Estep to investigate the haunted locations before he writes about them? "I love the storytelling process and that begins with the research and the 'boots on the ground' component of paranormal investigation," he said. "It's one thing to tell ghost stories you've gotten from interviewing witnesses. It's another thing entirely to spend a week living, sleeping, and investigating in the place you're writing about. I think it adds credibility."

Unlike most authors of historical-based ghost books, Estep tends to gravitate toward single locations—like Malvern Manor in Iowa or Asylum 49 in Utah—boasting enough ghostly material to sustain an entire book. "As my writing career progresses, I enjoy devoting an entire book to a single location," he said. "It feels as though the story has more room to breathe over the space of fifty thousand words than it does when it's compressed into a single chapter. I become very fond of some of the locations I investigate and like to delve into the lives of those who lived and worked there."

In the interview, Estep talked about his investigation at Fort Mifflin in Philadelphia and commented about the ghosts still lingering in the battlefields outside of the "Cradle of Liberty." The British are coming? According to Estep, the spirits of the fallen redcoats are still here, fighting against their rebel adversaries in the afterlife.

Q: Are the ghosts associated with battles more residual or intelligent based on your experience?
A: Most of my Revolutionary War experiences are from Fort Mifflin. There's a mixture there. Some most certainly seem to be intelligent and willing to communicate with visitors. Others, though, are obviously the equivalent of recordings. You can't have that much bloodshed in such a small place without it leaving behind a psychic scar of some kind.

Q: During your investigation of Fort Mifflin in Philadelphia, what type of hauntings did you encounter?
A: There were several layers. I was surprised to encounter entities that seemed to come from the Revolutionary War period, the Civil War, and even some that may have been more contemporary in nature. During the Civil War, Mifflin was used to house prisoners from both sides, including political prisoners. As one of the continental United States' longest serving fortresses, Mifflin has layer upon layer of haunted history.

Q: Any idea why Fort Mifflin is so haunted?
A: I believe the intense emotion that comes with battle, plus the incarceration of prisoners in very cruel and squalid conditions, has generated a great deal of paranormal activity there. A constant stream of visitors helps provide a power supply that allows the activity to manifest.

Q: Do you think objects associated with the Revolutionary War relics and battle items have energy associated with them?
A: I believe that some, though by no means all, objects may be imbued with energies dating back to that time period. Those who are skilled at detecting such energies may be able to pick up on their presence, if they are so attuned. That would make such special objects a fascinating window into times long since gone.

Q: It's fascinating to me that you dressed as a redcoat when you investigated Fort Mifflin. Do you feel Revolutionary War reenactors trigger residual hauntings?
A: Reenactors help keep history alive. As such, they provide era cues—sights, sounds, smells, and more from the era they are recreating—that seem to trigger paranormal activity. It's almost as if the spirits flock to that which seems familiar to them, gravitating toward the sound of muskets and cannons, which may have been the last thing they heard on this earth.

Q: Revolutionary-era forts and battlefields seem to be hotbeds of paranormal activity. Why?
A: It was an extremely contentious and emotional war. Young British redcoats not to mention German lads dying far from home, fighting for a cause they barely understood, let alone believed in. Americans who had traveled to the New World in order to escape the tyranny of the old, only to have it follow them in the form of the world's most ruthlessly efficient military machine, the British Army—cut down in the fields of their new home by the disciplined musketry of Cornwallis's men. There's a recipe for tragedy if ever you saw one, and where one finds tragedy, one also finds ghosts.

Q: Why do spirits from the Revolutionary War still linger?
A: Unfinished business, perhaps? Those Brits who died far from home may well be trapped, unsure of how to move on. Men who die in battle leave their bodies confused and terrified, which some say affects the ability of the spirit to transition. They may be in need of spiritual rescue or help with crossing over.

SHUTTERED SPIRITS OF '76

Who better to tell that story than the spirits of those who lived through it?

—Tim Weisberg, *Spooky Southcoast*

For a few months during the summer of 2018, I served as a docent at the Shirley-Eustis House located in the Roxbury neighborhood of Boston, Massachusetts. And, yes, my short stint giving tours of the historic property was spirited to say the least.

Built in 1747 by William Shirley, the Royal Governor of the Province of Massachusetts Bay, the property was occupied by Colonel Asa Witcomb's Sixth Foot Regiment later to be seized and sold as a Loyalist property in 1778.

The mansion sat vacant for several years until William Eustis, a congressman who also served as the secretary of war under James Madison's presidency during the War of 1812, acquired the house with his wife, Caroline Langdon Eustis.

As soon as I walked into the Georgian-style mansion nicknamed "Shirley Place" by its previous owners, I was contacted by the female spirit of the house, Madam Eustis. She whispered what

The Shirley-Eustis House in Boston, Massachusetts. *Photo by Frank C. Grace*

sounded like my name in my left ear. I then started to communicate with her using my copper dowsing rods.

The matriarch of the Shirley-Eustis House let me know in no uncertain terms that she didn't like some of the furniture in the first-floor "drawing room" and also seemed desperate to find out what happened to a painting that was removed after she passed in 1865. For the record, the mansion was divided into fifty-three units and sold two years after her death. Her artwork and a majority of her belongings were auctioned off by 1867.

The room where Eustis and his wife entertained visitors like the Marquis de Lafayette in 1824 and other luminaries like John Quincy Adams, Henry Clay, Daniel Webster, and Aaron Burr still features a replica of the famed portrait of William Eustis painted in 1804. The original by Gilbert Stuart is owned by the Metropolitan Museum of Art in Manhattan.

While working as a tour guide at the mansion, I encountered the ghost of Madam Eustis on a regular basis. She seemed to linger in the drawing room, solemnly looking out of the window facing what was her sanctuary, the estate's orchard and gardens. Based on the spirit's point of view, she could also see the historic carriage house, salvaged from Isabella Stewart Gardner's property in Brookline.

One Sunday afternoon, I decided to check out the off-limits attic of the mansion. There was a room known as the "Prophet's Chamber," which was used as a makeshift recovery room for bedridden victims of the Revolutionary War. As I was inspecting the weathered attic, I noticed pieces of what looked like original yellow wallpaper and signs of a fire indicated by the scorch marks on the historic wooden beams.

I also spotted a stain on the wall that clearly resembled a bloody handprint. Was it paint or something more sinister?

During the American Revolution, the Sixth Foot Regiment occupied the house. Meanwhile, Eustis was an up-and-coming surgeon. In fact, he served under Dr. Joseph Warren who was fatally wounded at the Battle of Bunker Hill. Eustis was also a known "spunker," or a member of a secret group of Harvard medical students known to steal cadavers used for anatomy dissections in medical school.

While it's rumored Eustis may have practiced medicine at the mansion, it's my guess the bloody handprint was left from one of the soldiers recovering in the "Prophet's Chamber" during the War of Independence.

The Shirley-Eustis House had many secrets. And, based on my interactions with Madam Eustis, I knew the spirits had answers to a few of the mansion's mysteries.

When I was approached by the lead docent to come up with ideas to generate much needed revenue to help with the preservation efforts of the estate, I suggested candlelight ghost tours or paranormal investigations.

She loved the idea and pitched it to the interim executive director. The response, however, was less than favorable. I was pulled into a closed-door meeting by one of the members from the Board of Governors. The volunteer treasurer mocked the idea saying sarcastically that she "talked with the ghosts of the house and they asked to be left alone." She also said the board wouldn't approve the ghost tours, which were to be led by battery-operated lanterns, because of the additional electricity costs.

After the uncomfortable meeting, the lead docent was let go from her job and I quickly resigned from a position I genuinely loved. The experience left me with even more unanswered questions. It didn't make sense. Why?

I reached out to an old college friend, Darrell Morrone, who now lives in Hartford, Connecticut. "They feel it brings down the

The spirit of Madam Eustis is said to leer out of the window located in the mansion's drawing room. *Photo by Frank C. Grace*

historical aspect, which I don't personally agree with," he told me. "I think having something intriguing about a location adds to it. Living in a town known as the Heartbeat of the Revolution, you can still hear the sounds of Lafayette and his men camping on the town green, the clink of metal cooking plates, and tent flaps in the breeze. But it's never spoken about in town for fear of impacting the sacred history of the location."

If a ghost is history demanding to be remembered, then why are some heritage organizations so apprehensive about opening their doors to paranormal-themed tours and investigations?

Michelle Hamilton, manager of the Mary Washington House in Fredericksburg, Virginia, and author of *Civil War Ghosts*, told me the answer is as diverse as each historical site. "One reason is that the paranormal is a belief system, either you believe in ghosts or you don't," she said. Hamilton added that religious beliefs play a huge part in the decision whether or not heritage organizations will open their doors to investigative teams. "Many view ghost tours and investigations as being disrespectful of the dead," she explained, "that ghost tours make money from the suffering of the dead."

Hamilton said the myths and misconceptions perpetuated by ill-informed guides doesn't help the cause. "A focus on diligent historic research in the field beyond just capturing another EVP saying, 'Get out!' will help improve the reputation of paranormal investigators," she said. "Another concern expressed by historical organizations is that the museum or property will become only known for its ghosts. The fear is that the site will become akin to a fun house attraction," Hamilton told me. "Also there's a risk of damage or vandalism to an historic site by investigators or the public."

Hamilton has a point. In recent years, however, there seems to be a noticeable shift among heritage organizations to become more open-minded about their resident ghosts while embracing the haunted history of the property they oversee.

One example of a location that has traditionally been tight-lipped about its spirits but has opened up a bit in recent years is the USS *Constitution*. During a visit I had in 2015, I noticed a dramatic shift when it comes to the staff's willingness to talk about its ghosts.

Launched in 1797 and often referred to as "Old Ironsides" because of its uncanny ability to repel shots fired during wartime

Staircase of the Oliver House in Middleboro, Massachusetts. *Photo by Frank C. Grace*

battles, the massive wooden-hulled, three-masted frigate serves as the United States Navy's official ambassador and is a throwback to the glory days of the War of 1812, when Old Ironsides defeated five British warships and captured numerous merchant vessels.

According to naval officer Wesley Bishop during my visit in 2015, the team from TV's *Ghost Hunters* was about to investigate the oldest commissioned naval vessel still afloat. And yes, the uniformed crew did strongly believe that Old Ironsides is, in fact, haunted. "No enemy died on board, so if there are ghosts, they're my fellow crew members who died long ago from battle-related wounds or the elements," Bishop told me. "I haven't had an encounter, but several of my (living) crew members have."

Meanwhile, his fellow naval officer friend chimed in, "There are definitely ghosts on board."

While I was peeking into the berthing area known as "the rack," I swore I saw a shadow figure dart by me. Of course, multiple reports have been made of a sailor wearing a navy blue jacket and gold buttons. Ellen MacNeil, who has investigated the USS *Constitution* with her team, S.P.I.R.I.T.S. of New England, confirmed the vessel is paranormally active.

"Is it haunted? Oh, hell yes," MacNeil told *Ghosts of the American Revolution*. Her team investigated *Constitution* in 2010 over a two-day period. "We totally freaked out the captain with our audio and video evidence. With 308 deaths on the ship, mainly from illness not battle, the ship is very much loved and protected by these lost souls who were playful, curious, and responsive to us being there."

As a featured stop on Boston's highly trafficked Freedom Trail, USS *Constitution* greets thousands of tourists daily and is a floating national treasure. It is, in essence, living naval history. However, this isn't a history that lies in a shallow grave. The blood of the fallen sailors that once stained the deck of the two-centuries-old frigate may have washed away over time, but the supernatural imprint of the Old Ironsides' casualties of war allegedly continue to haunt the legendary vessel.

According to former crew members, USS *Constitution* is a bonafide ghost ship. "We took ghosts so seriously on the *Constitution*," said Pete Robertson, a first-class petty officer who served aboard the vessel from 2001 to 2004, in an interview with *Stars and Stripes*. "Unless you were a brand-new crew member, you didn't mess around with that stuff. You didn't make jokes about it. . . . You didn't even try to scare each other because people were terrified. A lot of people were terrified to stand watch on the ship."

Robertson remembered seeing objects, like a twenty-four-pound cannonball, mysteriously moving on deck, despite the ship being completely still. "It was moving in ways a cannonball just shouldn't move," he said, adding that the odd motion was scientifically inexplicable.

Allie Thorpe, a former seaman serving between 2002 and 2005, echoed Robertson's experiences with paranormal activity while on board. "It would feel like there was somebody there with you," Thorpe explained. "It would feel like somebody was walking up behind you and blowing on your neck."

In an attempt to investigate the reports of alleged spirits, Lieutenant Commander Allen R. Brougham set up a camera overlooking *Constitution*'s wheel one evening in 1955. "At about midnight, the figure of a nineteenth-century navy captain appeared long enough to be captured on film," one report claimed. "The picture shows a man in gold epaulets reaching for his sword."

Spirits on deck? It would hardly be surprising. As a major player in a series of nineteenth-century maritime battles, *Constitution*'s shiny façade has been marred by the blood of former tenants.

Dorothy Burtz Fiedel, author of *Ghosts and Other Mysteries*, recounted a particularly dark chapter in Old Ironsides' history dating back to December 1884, when forty-three crew members became ill with fever and dysentery. Several died, including one man who was found on deck trying to crawl to the sick bay. In addition to the American naval casualties, several of the ship's prisoners of war were fatally wounded, including Captain Henry Lambert from the British Royal Navy, who was annihilated by a musket ball and passed away from his injuries on January 3, 1813.

Fiedel interviewed former crew members, and a few talked about a haunted cot suspended by chains in the ship's sleeping section, or the berthing area known as the rack. "Apparently, some of the sailors, who got stuck with that particular rack, refused to sleep in it and slept on the floor. One sailor, who braved the rack, woke up in the middle of the night . . . and he beheld the disembodied head of a normal-sized man. The face was pale, lifeless looking and . . . the form faded out around the neck area." One man encountered a phantom falling from the crow's nest, while others, similar to Officer Robertson's account in *Stars and Stripes*, heard cannonballs rolling around on deck, even though they were all welded together.

Gary Kent, a former crew member on the *Constitution* in the 1980s, described one late-night incident involving a residual haunting of a man dressed in an old-school uniform: "His jacket was black-bluish in color with gold buttons. . . . I immediately noticed the blood on his face. He had blood on his jacket." Kent said the three other men in the rack also saw the apparition, which he described as "foggy, frosty, and fuzzy," before it faded away.

While Kent's recollection of the ghostly sailor has lost its fear factor over time, the former officer said he is haunted by one strange thing he observed while serving on the *Constitution*: "Birds never landed on the ship. . . . There were a lot of high places for them to perch, but I never saw one land. I was very new to ships. . . . The old-timers, though, they thought it was very strange. . . . It was very strange, definitely not normal."

Incidentally, Kent's account of a sailor wearing a navy-blue jacket with gold buttons mirrors the image found in a photo taken by Lieutenant Captain Brougham in 1955. According to lore, the ghostly figure is a residual spirit of Commodore Thomas Truxton, the first man to command the *Constitution* in the late 1700s. He was known as a particularly harsh disciplinarian who reportedly tortured and murdered one sailor, Seaman Neil Harvey, after he fell asleep while manning the ship's deck. The murder was brutal; Harvey was stabbed in the gut, tied over the ship's cannon and blown to smithereens.

Perhaps Harvey's spirit is responsible for mysteriously moving the cannonballs on the ship's deck and waking up crew members in the wee hours of the night. Maybe it's a supernatural warning meant to protect the sleeping sailors from a fate worse than death—being tied to the end of *Constitution*'s loaded cannon and blown into a thousand little pieces while all hands on deck watch in horror.

Of course, not all heritage groups are so forthcoming as the USS *Constitution* when it comes to the paranormal.

Tim Weisberg, host of *Spooky Southcoast* and researcher for several TV shows, including *Haunted Towns* and *Ghost Stalkers*, told me he's encountered a few roadblocks over the years from several historical groups.

"For a region so integral to the history of our country, it seems as though the paranormal is not an acceptable topic for a majority of historic sites and heritage organizations," Weisberg said. "One of the main reasons for that, I believe, is that there is an 'old guard' that oversees many of these locations. They're people who got involved in preserving history decades ago, and they see paranormal research as an affront to what it is they've been doing all of these years. It's considered tacky and gives off the wrong impression, they'll tell you."

Weisberg believes New England's closed-minded Puritan ethos may be responsible for the "no ghost" mentality. "In actuality, the paranormal is how these sites will find the next generation of stewards," he said. "Young people are more interested in the haunts than the history, and someone needs to be ready to take over these sites or they'll fall by the wayside. Why not embrace the ghosts if it means someone will ensure the location lives on?"

When asked why some groups welcome the paranormal while others are less enthusiastic, Weisberg believes money is a huge factor. "Those who understand that allowing paranormal investigations of their historic sites could lead to new fundraising avenues are usually the ones most willing to let us in," he said. "The other factor is if the docents and employees are having their own paranormal experiences and they actually think the place is haunted,

Several spirits are believed to haunt the Oliver House, including Sally Hutchinson and her cat, Marigold. *Photo by Frank C. Grace*

they're more apt to allow us in so we can help them further explore what's been happening to them."

There has also been a shift with paranormal-themed shows, like *The Holzer Files* and programs he's worked on including *Haunted Towns*, to dig deep with the research and accurately portray the backstories of the historic locations. Weisberg's motto at the events he has hosted has been "come for the haunts, stay for the history," which echoes the latest trend from the paranormal pop culture emphasizing historical accuracy on TV and radio shows.

"The key is to show these organizations that as much as we're looking to capture data on investigations that may or may not prove the existence of ghosts, it's still one of our primary goals to accurately share and understand the history of these locations," Weisberg said. "Who better to tell that story than the spirits of those who lived through it?"

When I asked my friends in the paranormal community to direct me to a Revolutionary War–era location that successfully showcases its history and ghosts, almost all of them pointed to the Peter Oliver House in Middleboro, Massachusetts.

In the past, I've investigated the green shuttered home boasting more than 250 years of forgotten history. During my first visit in 2019, I was amazed by the layers of paranormal activity still lingering throughout the property, which included its original Loyalist owners, Dr. Peter Oliver and his wife Sally Hutchinson Oliver. The newlywed couple were forced out of their home when the Sons of Liberty confiscated the house in 1775. The revolutionaries auctioned off their valuables and then used the money to fund the American Revolution.

Christy Parrish, the house manager and event coordinator, told me the Oliver Estate's story is an important part of American history for both Middleboro and the nation as a whole. As someone oversees the estate, she understands why some regional heritage organizations are apprehensive about opening their historic properties to paranormal investigations.

"It's a full-time business," Parrish said. "When we first came into Middleboro and started offering ghost tours, we thought it might fizzle out. We didn't expect it would continue to build and the story would continue to grow and the energies here would learn to trust us."

Paranormal investigators captured an EVP of a conversation in the Oliver House's dining room. *Photo by Frank C. Grace*

Parrish gets why certain groups have closed their shutters to ghost tours and investigators "because there are teams that aren't serious about helping move a location's history forward," she said. "They're more interested in pushing their own agendas, which could be very harmful and set the paranormal field back."

The manager said the volunteers leading the investigations at the Oliver House have been handpicked "not by the town, but by the house," she said. "When we bring in a volunteer, we wait it out and see how the house reacts to them. We've been successful here because this house was in a lot worse shape than it is today. We continue to thrive because of the tours and the honest approach we take."

The Oliver House's manager explained that it's important for heritage organizations to accurately showcase the property's history, even if it's sympathetic to the Loyalist perspective. "We teach people in a very respectful way how to talk to history," she said.

Because of this less combative approach, the spirits have opened up to the Oliver House's volunteer staff. In one bone-chilling recording captured by the team, a female spirit clearly whispered, "They won't let us speak" in the dining room area. Also captured in the EVP audio recording was a male spirit calling the woman's comments "rubbish" and then the dominant male voice mentioned a "Mr. Adams," believed to be Samuel Adams.

Parrish said the female spirits of the house refuse to be silenced from beyond the grave. "We give them a platform to be heard, so their affairs and feelings can be understood," she said. "We're bringing their personalities to the forefront of the ghost tours. We offer the spirits here something that they didn't have during the Revolutionary War era. We give them a voice."

TOWN CRIER Q&A: CHRISTY PARRISH

The Oliver House is a shining example of the resilience of the human spirit.

—Christy Parrish, Oliver House

There's no denying that Christy Parrish, the Oliver House's event coordinator and manager, has a deep, heartfelt connection with Sally Hutchinson. "I'm pretty in tune with her," Parrish said, adding that Hutchinson "is a fairly complicated woman."

In fact, Parrish believes she may have an inexplicable spiritual tie with Mrs. Peter Oliver, the daughter of the British governor of Massachusetts Bay and the first lady of the house on Plymouth Street in Middleboro, Massachusetts.

"There was a psychic who had a conversation with Andrew Oliver and he told her I was his brother's daughter-in-law and that I once lived here," Parrish recalled. "I laughed when he said that because that would mean my soul has somehow traveled through time and that I'm a modern version of Sally."

After a bizarre experience she had trance channeling Hutchinson's spirit, Parrish now believes it's a viable explanation as to why she's so drawn to the historic property. "I have a loyalty and duty

Christy Parrish. *Photo by Frank C. Grace*

to save the Oliver House and I can't explain where it comes from," she said. "I somehow know so much more about Sally that I rarely share. It's almost as if it's instinctual."

In the interview, Parrish talked about the lingering legacy associated with Thomas Hutchinson's daughter and the other Revolutionary War–era spirits still hanging out at the Oliver House including an agitated male entity, a flirty chambermaid, and several sightings of an orange tabby named Marigold.

Yes, the Oliver House even has a resident ghost cat with a tale to tell. Or is it tail?

Q: Why has history overlooked eighteenth-century figures like Sally Hutchinson?
A: Women were not as vocal nor were they allowed to voice their opinions in those times. They were expected to run their households, raise their children, and stand by their husbands. It's possible that Sally has been overlooked because of her loyalty to the crown. When she was born, she followed suit and her family's bloodline was Loyalist. She came from privilege and lived in the upper crust of society. It could be that the community viewed her as a rich, spoiled woman and simply had no interest in getting to know her.

When the Revolution started to escalate, she began to feel the unwelcoming sentiment of the general population. It can be easy to overlook people if we pay no attention to them. Ignoring them takes away their power. She grew up in a time of unrest and harsh feelings that were directed toward the Loyalists. She simply didn't have a choice in being a Tory.

Q: What are some of the Oliver House hauntings with ties to the era?
A: The activity in the house is intense and the Oliver family is heavily imprinted on the location. There have been solid, full-bodied apparitions that appear throughout the home, and the beauty of this is they are revealing the story of what actually happened. There are two chambermaids, Julie and Sarah, both around sixteen years old.

Julie has appeared and been witnessed by multiple people on different occasions. She would have been the chambermaid who serviced Peter's side of the home. When she first started to manifest, she revealed herself during an event. She appeared in the bedroom closet connected to Peter's room. Our volunteer, Chris Andrade, walked through the closet into the back bedroom and then upon her return she saw a girl in the closet behind the clothes that were hanging there. Julie locked eyes with the volunteer, and quickly placed her finger to her lips urging Chris to be quiet. Next, Julie took a step back and disappeared into the wall. We were able to determine the names of the various energies at the house during our investigations. Multiple people have seen Julie and describe her the same as what Chris had witnessed.

Sarah was Sally Hutchinson's chambermaid. The interesting thing about Sarah is that she's a flirt. People experience Sarah throughout the house. She likes to drop the temperature and blow on men's necks. We have captured her voice numerous times through the years and she always seems to gravitate toward the male visitors.

Q: What about Peter Oliver's uncle, Andrew?
A: Andrew Oliver, Peter's uncle, has been very heavy-handed in the house. Interactions with Andrew Oliver primarily happen in the Benjamin Franklin room on the first floor of the house. Andrew was one of the authors of the letters that were removed from the house and eventually given to the Sons of Liberty. These letters contributed to the quick downfall of the family.

Andrew is often captured on audio. There are times when you can actually hear the conversations happening between two men in the house.

Q: How prevalent is Sally Hutchinson Oliver's spirit in the house?
A: She has been witnessed countless times. She usually appears beautifully dressed. What's interesting is her dress is different from time to time. The first evidence of Sally in the house was when a guest photographed her apparition at the top of the staircase. She smells of lavender when she is near. When Sally is present, people express this overwhelming feeling of sadness, especially while in her bedroom we lovingly call the Hutchinson chamber. Her energy continues to grow stronger and stronger now that she's allowed to have a voice.

Sally had a pet, an orange tabby called Marigold. The cat appears in solid form and lingers upstairs in Sally's room. The cat has been captured on audio by various teams and witnessed on countless occasions. One of the guests experienced Marigold rubbing against his leg while he was in the Hutchinson chamber. The first appearance of the cat happened during the set up for an event when two volunteers headed toward Sally's room and the tabby jumped off the bed and ran into the fireplace. The cat just disappeared.

Q: It's said the seeds of the American Revolution started at the Oliver House. What exactly happened to earn that reputation?
A: When the mob surrounded the house in 1775, Sally, Peter, and their two sons fled to Boston with only the clothes on their backs. They could find safety in the city as it was occupied heavily with British forces and General Gage. The rebels started to strip the house. Every item was confiscated and carefully inventoried. All of the family's belongings were sold and the Sons of Liberty were able to take that money and buy ammunition to fight the war for freedom from the British crown. And the twist to this is that they purchased musket balls manufactured at Oliver Mill, the prosperous mill that was formerly owned by Judge Peter Oliver.

It's also believed the Sons of Liberty held secret meetings inside the home as they planned their attack.

Q: What did the Sons of Liberty do with the house after they ransacked it and any hauntings associated with the Patriots?
A: After the house was confiscated, it would become the property of the Commonwealth. There are the sounds of heavy boots people experience when they visit the house, and one can't help but wonder if the smell of fresh tobacco isn't a sign of the Sons of Liberty's occupation of the home. There's a phantom sound of a musket firing experienced a few times every year. The house begins to feel anxious when we hear the gunshots and you can feel the tension build.

We're still just scraping the surface of the stories retold by the energies. But it wouldn't be beyond the realm of possibility that we will begin to hear from the rebels as time goes on.

Q: Did Benjamin Franklin actually visit the Oliver House?
A: In 1773, Benjamin Franklin was invited to party at Oliver Hall, which was later burned down by the revolutionaries. Judge Peter Oliver writes in his journal about Ben visiting and staying at the hall. Ben was invited so the family could get a better idea about the leader's loyalties. They needed a strong, persuasive individual on their side to help bring the dissension to an end, so they would try to win him over during the course of his stay.

Thomas Hutchinson was also present during the party and since his daughter's house was close, Thomas would visit Sally and Peter at what was called the Small Oliver House. It's completely possible Benjamin Franklin visited the house with Thomas. But during the visit it's unlikely he rummaged through Sally's personal belongings. Thomas had hidden twenty letter packets in his daughter's room. What did happen, and this cannot be disputed, is that Benjamin Franklin did obtain possession of the letters while he was there.

Through our investigations, we've been told by the energies of the home that it was the servants who were able to get those letters to Franklin and they were paid well for the transaction. It would make sense that Franklin was in the house, however, he wouldn't have gone upstairs. He would have stayed in the main parlor where business was conducted and it was at that moment life would change forever for both the Oliver and the Hutchinson families. There would be no turning back.

Q: There are reports of shadow figures in the basement. What's the backstory with the cellar dwellers?
A: We believe the shadow figures in the basement are those who were enslaved. We are unclear about the time frame and they are pretty evasive about answering questions, so hopefully in time we will be able to get more clarity.

Q: Are there secrets associated with the Oliver House that have yet to be uncovered?
A: There are many secrets within this house. Some of it is information we've uncovered while trying to understand the truth associated with the individuals who lived here.

There are objects we have discovered and still more to be found. Yes, we have been given information regarding some of the objects and we do believe wholeheartedly that when the timing is right and it is the right person, then discoveries will be made.

They have shown us several locations, so time will tell what we will uncover. Whatever we find always remains at the house because it's their property. Our level of respect for the energies of the Oliver House and their mutual trust is more valuable to us than any monetary value associated with a discovered object.

Q: How has the Oliver House shaped your views regarding the paranormal?

A: The Oliver House is a shining example of the resilience of the human spirit. The activity within the walls paints a picture that sometimes is—and sometimes isn't—exactly how it's written or explained to us. Discovering the characters and feeling their sadness, joy, and fear are extremely important to building a level of respect and open communication with the Oliver House's spirits.

It goes beyond turning on a piece of equipment. The beauty comes from those fleeting moments when we are able to feel, smell, see, and hear them and to create a comfort level that transcends time. Though there are many layers to the hauntings at the Oliver House, we're privileged to be the ones with whom they share their truths and, in return, we will try our best to do right by them and share their stories with others.

Christy Parrish embodies the sadness of the Oliver House's first lady, Sally Hutchinson. *Photo by Frank C. Grace*

CONCLUSION

Similar to the cursed legacy associated with the Salem witch trials hysteria of 1692, the American Revolution is stained with blood and its ghosts are still lurking in the shadows seeking postmortem revenge.

In November 2017, I signed on to be a night auditor, an overnight front-desk employee, for a new boutique hotel that opened up on Essex Street in Salem, Massachusetts. The historic building had a past life as Newmark's Department Store. Because there was only a skeleton crew during the graveyard shift, I had to do some work downstairs in the under-construction basement such as making coffee and folding laundry. The lower level is also where the filled-in, subterranean tunnel connecting the Daniel Low building was located.

My first paranormal experience at the hotel involved what looked like a cloud like black mass that emerged from the right-hand elevator on the first floor of the hotel. I could see it clearly from the front desk. One evening, I caught a glimpse of the shadow hovering near the elevator and then I heard what sounded like someone violently kicking the doors. No surprise, but the elevator went off track.

A few weeks after that initial incident, I heard what sounded like someone taking a piece of metal and then taking a hammer and banging it next door while making coffee in the lower level, which was covered in tarps. It was around 3:00 a.m. in January 2018 and the lights in the basement started to flicker. I then heard what sounded like a man in pain. He was moaning and not in a good way.

I ran upstairs thinking it was someone outside. Because I'm friends with the owners, I looked into the window of the independent bookstore on Essex Street to make sure no one was trying to break into the store. I started to pray.

While I was peeking through the windows, I saw what looked like a shadow in the shape of a man dart by in the window of Wicked Good Books. The entity seemed to be wearing a hat. The figure then stopped and looked at me. It was almost as if the shadow man was communicating with me telepathically:

You see me? Yes, I can see you.

When we made eye contact for the first time, I saw something that continues to scar my psyche. It still horrifies me to think about what I saw that night. The man with a hat had red, glowing eyes.

Could it be an employee, perhaps, working a late-night shift? I gasped for air and looked again in disbelief. It was gone. I felt frozen during this encounter, as if I was having a face-to-face interaction with my worst nightmare. Seconds after making contact with the entity, I heard what sounded like a blood-curdling scream echo from the alley next to Rockefellas located in the Daniel Low building. When I ran down Essex Street to investigate, there was nobody there.

I was hoping it was an explanation like a reflection from the streetlights. The scream could have been an animal, like a stray cat. After several attempts to come up with a rational explanation, I was stumped. I was also paralyzed by fear. In fact, I ended up leaving my job at the hotel a few days after that incident because I was too creeped out to continue.

The following day, I asked the shop's manager if anybody was working a late-night shift. Nope.

The bookshop's co-owner, Denise Kent, believes it could be the spirit of one of the previous owners from that property in Derby Square. My theory? I think Salem is haunted. Period. The spirits that roam the streets and shops—including Wicked Good Books—come out during the winter. I believe the entity just made a pit stop at the bookstore that night.

Did I happen to stumble on this entity with red, glowing eyes by accident or was it reaching out to me specifically? If so, why me?

In hindsight, this initial face-to-face encounter with the shadow figure was the beginning of a series of terrifying encounters. Why was the inhuman entity stalking me? It was as if the man with a hat was lurking in the shadows of Salem and seeking justice from beyond the grave.

For me, the biggest challenge was trying to figure out if this was an inhuman entity or an angry spirit still lurking in the shadows of Salem. In other words, was this shadow figure ever a person?

Nearly two hundred men and women were accused during the Salem witch trials, and twenty innocents were executed for witchcraft in 1692. *Photo by Jason Baker*

Michael Robishaw, the shaman who successfully removed an attachment from me in 2016, said his spirit guides help him identify if it's actually the man with a hat when he's out in the field. "I've had many cases with this same entity being a real evil and nasty son of a gun," Robishaw told me. "It's a dark shadow type entity with very distinct traits."

The man with a hat generally manifests itself at night and is dressed in a long, black trench coat or a three-piece suit. He wears a hat, which has been different in various reports. Some say it's a fedora or a top hat. The entity I've seen in Salem wears what looks like a seventeenth-century reverend's hat and a long, black cloak. Some say the shadow person has red, glowing eyes and it's at least six feet tall.

When people have confronted the entity demanding it to reveal its name, several witnesses have reported the man with a hat said he was "Scratch," an old nickname for the devil himself.

Mike Ricksecker, author of *A Walk in the Shadows*, is a Cleveland-based paranormal researcher who specializes in the phenomena. He said the man with a hat is classified as a shadow person. "They're very mysterious," he told me. "They come in a lot of different forms so people commonly see the man with a hat wearing a fedora, top hat, and with a wide brim hat like Zorro. I've had one person tell me a story about a hat person wearing an archer's hat, like it was something out of Robin Hood."

Why so many different looks? "It's speculation, but maybe they're in disguise," he said. "I believe a true shadow person is an interdimensional being, so they're in and out of our plane of existence. They're also out of time, so it could mean a man wearing a fedora may have been around in the 1940s and, coming in during this time frame, not realizing things have changed. They also could be trying to impersonate someone from the 1940s. Are they trying to dupe us? I'm not sure."

When asked if the man with a hat lingers at locations with a history of violence and unjust killings, Ricksecker explained there are no geographic limitations. "I've gotten reports from all over," he said. "Sometimes people will report seeing a hat person at their house and I'm not sure if there was a murder at their house or if there was a Native American backstory to it. I would say that any location that has negative energy attached to it could certainly entice these things to come forward."

I mentioned to Ricksecker that the man with a hat entity I encountered in Salem seemed to be neither good nor bad. The shadow person appeared to be watching me and possibly feeding off of my energy. "There are people out there who automatically think a shadow person is evil and that's not the case," he said. "You mentioned it was a 'watcher' and a lot of times they're just looking at you. Yes, it's creepy. But it's not actually doing anything evil. I've even heard reports of it possibly being benevolent."

As far as the shadow person hierarchy, Ricksecker said the man with a hat seems to be a higher-echelon entity. He also said it's common for people to compartmentalize them as lower-level beings "because when they come into existence in our dimension as dark manifestations," he explained, "we automatically assume they are of a lower resonance. Some of these entities are what I call a pure shadow person and others are human spirits that can't fully manifest."

Could the man with a hat in Salem be what is known as a "thought form" or *tulpa*, which is an entity created through spiritual or mental powers? "There are enough people going to Salem who consistently recognize what happened back in 1692 like the witch trials and the hangings," he said. "There was a lot of innocent blood. People flock there every October for that very thing. Did a thought form come out of that and manifest into this entity or did another entity come along and decide to piggyback on those atrocities? Yes, it's possible."

Another explanation is that the man with a hat entity I encountered in Salem was somehow summoned from another dimension. "I've heard reports of the crawler type shadow person being conjured," he said. "They're related, and, based on their similarities, I would have to say it's definitely possible for the man with a hat to be conjured."

I asked Ricksecker if he thought the entity wearing a hat was actually a spirit of an actual person with ties to the Salem witch trials and not a shadow person. "Based on your description, I was wondering if it's a human spirit and what you're saying out loud is very personal to them," he said. "Maybe it's something they're ashamed of or history has been changed over time and there is misinformation."

Ricksecker then asked me if I had a gut feeling about the entity. I told him I was initially convinced the entity was once a person trying to manifest, however, it didn't fit the typical profile. In addition to wearing a hat, it also had red, glowing eyes. I've never seen anything like it before in the spirit realm.

Another side effect of my run-ins with the entity was feeling completely drained after each encounter. "When it comes to the man with a hat, it's usually what we call an energy vampire," he said. "Even though it might be standing there and watching you, these things are instilling that fear into you and it's feeding off of that fear. I'm not sure if you're frightened when you see this entity, but it does sound like it's feeding off of your energy."

Yes, I was initially terrified. In fact, I was frozen with fear. But I did notice when I tried to ignore the man with a hat entity, the encounters seemed to be less frequent.

Then it hit me. The first time I encountered the man with a hat entity back in January 2018, I also heard what sounded like a woman screaming.

The attic of the House of the Seven Gables, also known as the Turner-Ingersoll Mansion, is located in Salem, Massachusetts. *Photo by Frank C. Grace*

Could the man with a hat I encountered somehow be tied to the legend of Salem's Lady in the Blue Dress?

The story of the Essex Street's resident ghost has gotten more elaborate over the years, with some claiming the alleged murder victim was pregnant and she was meeting her suitor with the hopes that they would get married. According to the ever-changing legend, she was attacked as she was waiting for her beloved. While the perpetrator is different based on each retelling, I've also heard from various guides that her sailor boyfriend was the one who actually murdered her.

When I first started giving tours in Salem, I was told that the Lady in Blue was breaking up a fight with her boyfriend and another sailor. As she was trying to stop the quarrel, the young woman was accidentally killed. My take on the so-called tragedy is the man was alone with her and snapped when he heard she was pregnant with his baby. He then fatally bludgeoned the poor lady who supposedly wore a blue dress.

How the woman was murdered has been told differently over the years. Some tour guides believe she was hit over the head with a rock or slammed against a brick wall. Others claimed she was stabbed.

The accepted version of the tale, however, was that a woman was left for dead in the tunnel after she was accidentally shot. The men who killed her confessed their sin to the reverend of the First Church, who, years later burdened with the guilt of the knowledge of the murder, hanged himself in the top floor of the church, leaving a note detailing the crime. According to locals, the reverend is often seen haunting the second floor of the historic Daniel Low building—typically through the windows that face Essex Street.

After my initial encounter with the man with a hat in a window on Essex Street, I also heard a blood-curdling scream and my internal alarms kicked into high gear. It sounded like a woman crying for help and it was coming from the dark alley next to Rockafellas. I ran over to the Daniel Low building expecting to encounter someone being attacked. There was no one there.

When I recounted my face-to-face encounter with the shadow person on the Travel Channel's *Most Terrifying Places* in 2019, I also discussed a possible tie to the Blue Lady based on a creepy experience I had while working the overnight shift at the Hotel Salem on Essex Street. The boutique hotel is only a few blocks away from the Daniel Low building and I regularly passed by Rockefellas when I headed into work.

Looking back at the incident, I initially believed that the man with a hat was trying to tell me something. But what about the mysterious scream coming from the alley behind Rockafellas? I instinctually believe it's somehow tied to the Lady in the Blue Dress legend.

If that's the case, then it could be a residual haunting or videotaped replay of a traumatic event. There's also the possibility that it could be an actual earthbound spirit wearing what looked like a reverend's hat.

And, yes, it's possibly a *tulpa* conjured by someone else.

My demonologist friend, James Annitto, told me he believes whatever was stalking me in Salem has been hanging around the Witch City for hundreds of years. "Maybe it's interested in your energy or it's warning you," he said. "If it is the man with a hat, these entities are very

A memorial at Proctor's Ledge honors the twenty innocent victims of the witch trials in Salem. *Photo by Sam Baltrusis*

old and wise. In most situations, a peaceful resolution comes from an understanding that we can push the negative out with a higher power. The positive will always outweigh the negative."

What's going on and why am I being visited by this inhuman entity in Salem? I reached out to Jack Kenna, a paranormal investigator and author featured on TV shows like *Paranormal Survivor* and *Haunted Case Files*. He believes there's an inhuman entity lurking in the shadows of the Witch City and may be responsible for the ghostly visitations.

"There's something much older and much more intense that resides in the Salem area," Kenna told me. "It likes to pretend it is something other than it is, and while I would not call it demonic, I would say it has a dislike of humans and is something I would call elemental in its nature. In other words, it is non-human."

Kenna believes the Witch City has an "aura of disaster" that has left a psychic imprint. "Like most of New England, there is a lot of history in Salem," he said. "Some of its history is good and some very tragic."

The paranormal investigator said tragedies preceding the witch trials of 1692 stained the land with blood. "In 1615, the Naumkeag tribe engaged in war with the Tarrantine people, which cost the lives of many on both sides," he explained. "Then in 1617 a plague broke out in the region, which took a heavy toll on the Naumkeag people."

Kenna said the smallpox epidemic in the 1630s devastated Salem's native population, which tainted the soil in the years leading up to the witch trials. "Then in 1830 one of the most infamous murders in early American history took place in Salem, the murder of Captain Joseph White by Richard Crowninshield," he said. "If there ever was a town that had cause to be haunted it would be Salem."

The author of *S.P.I.R.I.T.S. of New England: Hauntings, Ghosts & Demons* said his empathic abilities are heightened in the Witch City. "Having spent some time in Salem in recent years and being able to participate in investigations at locations in town, I have picked up on something more than just human spirit and the residual energies of past events in these locations," he said.

What exactly is an "elemental" entity that Kenna believes is hiding in Salem's shadows? "They are an ancient inhuman spirit directly connected to the elements of our world . . . earth, wind, fire, and water," Kenna explained, adding that Native Americans worshipped these ancient elementals and they are still revered by native tribes. "They are not demons or angels. Elementals don't try to physically harm humans but they typically don't like modern humans because of the way we treat the world."

Yes, it would make sense that an elemental entity was lurking in the shadows of Salem.

In April 2019, I returned to Witch City to work for Salem Historical Tours. I met with the tour owner, Giovanni Alabiso, and he said a shadow figure was spotted in the office. In fact, he said a voice asked, "when is he coming back?" and he automatically assumed it somehow was related to me because of my reputation as the Witch City's ghost guy.

As the weeks progressed, Salem started to get progressively dark for me. A paper weight hurled off the shelf toward me one afternoon. My co-workers were shocked. Multiple tour guides reported seeing a black mist followed by a shadow figure wearing a hat in the office. "I heard something tonight and it sounded like it was behind me, but that would be the wall," Alabiso told me. "It sounded like a scraping noise. It wasn't me. I like the idea that the place has history and spirits, but it seems like this is becoming problematic."

The last straw for me was when I heard footsteps walk up the stairs leading to the office on Central Street. When I looked down near the front-entrance door, I saw that same shadow figure with the hat leering beneath the stairs. The activity was intensifying and I couldn't make it stop.

At this point, I felt like I was being stalked. The following week I decided to take a break. The short-term goal was to stop giving ghost tours until I figured out why I was being pushed out of Salem by this inhuman entity.

Then I received a phone call that literally turned my world upside down.

While I was publicly writing about the ghosts associated with the Salem witch trials of 1692, my mother in Florida was secretly navigating the complexities of the genealogy of my family's maternal side using Ancestry.com. It was the day after I launched my second book on the Witch City called *Wicked Salem* when my mother dropped the bombshell.

"It looks like our ancestors had something to do with burning those witches," she told me with her thick Southern accent. I kindly corrected her. "Mom, they were hanged, not burned. But what did you find?"

My heart dropped when she started to rattle off names I knew all too well. I'm a descendant of the Newport, Rhode Island, branch of the Gould family who migrated to the New World in the 1600s. At first, I thought we were in the clear. However, there was one Gould who played a pivotal role in the horrors that unfolded in Salem Village in 1692. My Puritan yeoman grandfather ten-times removed had a sister, Priscilla Gould, who married John Putnam in 1611. If you know anything about the witch-trials hysteria, you know the name Putnam.

My Salem secret is that I'm related to both the Putnam and Gould families who owned land in two cities, Danvers and Topsfield, located in what was then called Salem Village in Massachusetts.

What really caused the deadliest witch hunt in American history? People who go on my walking tours or hear me lecture know my opinion. Yep, my Putnam cousins were responsible. They did it. And their land is stained with the blood of twenty innocent people. Salty tears started to flow down my cheeks. My paranormal journey over the past decade—the scratches, the strange visitations, and ultimately the entity attachment in Topsfield featured on the Travel Channel's *A Haunting*—all made sense.

My family hunted witches.

How does this personal revelation about my bloodstained lineage apply to my *Ghosts of the American Revolution* book? In addition to being connected to the "bad guys" of the Salem witch trials including the afflicted Ann Putnam Jr. and her ringleader father Thomas, I also have ties to the side of the family who defied the status quo during the trials and signed the petition on behalf of their neighbor Rebecca Nurse.

Sadly, Nurse was hanged at Proctor's Ledge on July 19, 1692, but I did find some relief knowing I was also related to Joseph Putnam, the youngest brother of the persecuting Thomas. He was a witch-trials opponent and member of the "anti-Parris" village committee formed on October 16, 1691. He rallied against the reverend who led the congregation of what is now modern-day Danvers.

When the witch-trial examinations began, Joseph reportedly stormed over to his older brother's house and confronted the family. "If you dare to touch with your foul lies anyone belonging to my household," he told Ann Putnam Sr., "you shall answer for it." Joseph was on high alert after defending Nurse and challenging the supposedly afflicted finger pointers. In fact, he kept his horses saddled in case one of his immediate family members were accused. They never were.

I'm also related to a Revolutionary War hero.

Joseph's son Israel was born in 1718 and he ultimately became one of the nation's most beloved generals during the War of Independence. Based on several accounts, my distant cousin was a colorful leader to say the least.

Author Sam Baltrusis has penned two books on the Witch City, including *Wicked Salem: Exploring Lingering Lore and Legends. Photo by Frank C. Grace*

Only about five feet and six inches tall, Israel Putnam was a local legend even before the American Revolution. "Old Put," as he was called by his peers, moved from Salem Village to Pomfret, Connecticut, in 1740 and became a successful farmer.

He was an outspoken member of the Sons of Liberty and was responsible for leading an angry mob that forced Andrew Oliver to resign from his post as a stamp agent. His crew burned the Loyalist in effigy after the Stamp Act was enacted. Yes, Oliver quickly quit his job to avoid a conflict.

Putnam also responded in his typical over-the-top theatrics when he heard that Thomas Gage, the military governor of Massachusetts, had seized gunpowder stored in modern-day Somerville, Massachusetts. He rallied together a group of about a thousand men from Connecticut to march toward Boston in a pre-war demonstration known as the Powder Alarm.

When he learned about the "shot heard round the world" in Concord and Lexington, he reportedly left his plow in the field and jumped on his horse. He made the trip from Pomfret to Cambridge, which is about a 100 mile trek, in little over eighteen hours.

After his stint with the Sons of Liberty, he was named a major general of the Continental Army and was second behind the commander-in-chief, George Washington. In the days leading up to the Battle of Bunker Hill, he rallied the troops to combat British General William Howe's plan to siege Boston. The famous one-line command, "don't fire until you see the whites of their eyes," has been attributed to him, but it's believed to be more legend than fact.

Putnam did, however, care deeply about the welfare of his "brave lads," as he called his men, and inspired them to persevere and fight for the cause. "Americans are not at all afraid of their heads, though very much afraid of their legs," he said before the epic battle on Breed's Hill. "If you cover these, they will fight forever."

Putnam was put in charge of New York City's military operations until Washington arrived and later commanded troops in Princeton, New Jersey, from January to May 1777. He was forced to retire in 1779 after having a stroke. He died near his home in Brooklyn, Connecticut, on May 29, 1790. He was seventy-two years old.

When I mentioned I was related to Putnam to my friend Peter Muise, he pointed out a legend that preceded the general's rise to fame during the American Revolution. Muise wrote about an incident that happened in 1742 when Putnam first moved to Pomfret, Connecticut. "A she-wolf lived on the outskirts of town, and she and her pups frequently ravaged the town's livestock," Muise wrote in a *New England Folklore* blog post. "The townspeople had been able to trap and kill all her children, but the she-wolf herself always escaped their snares."

Muise said Putnam tracked down the wolf found in a cave near his property. After hearing the animal growl, he asked his neighbor to tie a rope around his ankle as he descended into the abyss. "As he reached the end of the cave he could see the wolf's eyes shining in the torchlight. It growled menacingly," Muise recounted. "Putnam realized he had left his rifle outside, so he pulled on the rope. His neighbors pulled him out as fast as they could, dragging him across the sharp stones and ripping his clothes."

Covered in blood, Putnam grabbed his rifle and climbed back into the cave. He fired one shot and the neighbor slowly pulled him out of the tight space. Putnam had slayed the wolf.

"It was the last wolf ever seen in Connecticut, but it sounds like its ghost is still lurking around," Muise explained. "Israel Putnam's ghost is also supposedly still lurking around the area and is seen most frequently in the building where his funeral was held."

The story reminded me of an inexplicable experience I had involving what looked like a wolf spirit with piercing, gold-and-green eyes. At the time, I had learned from my mother about the family's connections to the Putnam family and I was agonizing over the idea I was related to the bad guys from the Salem witch trials.

After having a nightmare one night, I woke up and saw what looked like two eyes peering at me next to my bed. It looked like the ghostly outline of a wolf and then disappeared after I grabbed my glasses. Oddly, I wasn't scared. In fact, the bedside visitation had a calming effect. In hindsight, I believe my colorful cousin was sending me a sign from beyond the grave. Was "Old Put" paying me a visit? Yes, I'm convinced.

ACKNOWLEDGMENTS

If a ghost is history demanding to be remembered, then the spirits rumored to hang out at Old North Bridge where the American Revolution first erupted on April 19, 1775, are in hibernation.

Yes, they're taking a "boo" break.

During a series of off-season visits where the "shot heard round the world" was fired, I was surprised that many of the historical locations in Concord and Lexington—like Buckman Tavern and the Battle Green—had very few reports of ghostly activity. One tour guide in Lexington supposedly spotted an apparition of a colonial-era woman on the Buckman Tavern's second floor and another person swore they heard phantom footsteps at the Sanderson House.

Apparently, all of the nearby Revolutionary War's spirits headed over to Concord's Colonial Inn, which seems to be the area's most haunted location. Yes, it's a ghost hotel where spirits check in, but don't check out.

The "shot heard round the world" was fired at the Old North Bridge in Concord, Massachusetts. *Courtesy Deposit Photos*

On a whim, I spent one more overnight at the haunted inn as I finished up writing this book. After checking into Concord's Colonial Inn in early March, I decided to take a midnight stroll down the street to the Old North Bridge, the location where the first shots were fired that ultimately ignited the powder keg known as the American Revolution.

The full moon over Concord made the evening visit creepier than expected. As I approached the historic site, I heard what sounded like heavy footsteps marching over the bridge as if they were walking over to me. No one was there. What was even more strange with the situation was that the phantom footsteps stormed right by me as if they didn't even know I was there.

Residual redcoats? Yes, Concord has them.

Based on my encounter at the Old North Bridge, there's no denying that an inexplicable energy continues to linger where it all began. Based on several reports and my first-hand experiences, however, the spirits seem to be residual in nature.

According to Brian J. Cano, these types of playback hauntings fade over time, but can be exacerbated by the living. "We're constantly expending energy and leaving bits of ourselves behind," Cano told me. "These sorts of things are the basic building blocks of an echo."

When Revolutionary War performers replay the Battles of Lexington and Concord every April, Cano believes it could stir up the sleepy spirits. "Reenactors are very dedicated to their performances," he said. "When they're in uniform, they are out for blood and that energy can be left behind. The battle is replayed over and over again and I believe the spirits are reenergized because of it."

I'm grateful for all of the people I interviewed for this book in addition to Cano, including Joni Mayhan, Gare Allen, Peter Muise, Michelle Hamilton, Geoffrey Campbell, Christy Parrish, Tim Weisberg, Vicki Noel Harrington, Bill Pavao, James Annitto, Mike Ricksecker, Joe "Jiggy" Webb, Ellen MacNeil, Michael Baker, Gavin Kleespies, Christopher Rondina, and Richard Estep. Special thanks to Roxie Zwicker for penning the book's foreword. I would also like to thank the staff and front desk supervisor Zachary Trznadel at Concord's Colonial Inn for their continued hospitality while writing *Ghosts of the American Revolution*.

Photographers Frank C. Grace and Jason Baker deserve a supernatural slap on the back for capturing the eerie aesthetic of the main haunts featured in this book. I would also like to thank Amy Lyons from Globe Pequot for her support during the process of putting *Ghosts of the American Revolution* together.

Thanks to my mother, Deborah Hughes Dutcher, for her investigative work uncovering our familial ties to the Revolutionary War–era hero General Israel Putnam and my friends for their continued support.

Ghosts of the American Revolution is dedicated to my stepfather, Paul Dutcher, who passed on December 26, 2018. His love for American history and adventurous spirit lives on.

My goal was to give a voice to our founding fathers, unsung heroes, and, in a few cases, the British Loyalists featured in this book. *Ghosts of the American Revolution* is for them. I hope I do them justice.

SOURCES

Updated excerpts from my first thirteen books, including *Ghosts of Cambridge*, *13 Most Haunted in Massachusetts*, and *Haunted Boston Harbor* were featured in *Ghosts of the American Revolution*.

The material in this book is drawn from published sources, including my articles in *DigBoston* and issues of *Archaeology News Network*, *Austin's American-Statesman*, the *Berkshire Eagle*, *Boston Globe*, *Boston Herald*, *Boston Phoenix*, *The Enterprise*, the *Gloucester Telegraph*, *Harvard Crimson*, *Harvard Gazette*, *Herald News*, the *New York Times*, *North Andover's Eagle-Tribune*, *The Observer*, *Salem News*, *Salem Evening News*, *Smithsonian* magazine, *SouthCoast Today*, Zagat, and television programs such as Travel Channel's *Most Terrifying Places*, *Kindred Spirits*, *A Haunting*, and *Ghost Hunters* formerly on Syfy. The HISTORY Channel's three-part miniseries *Washington* served as a major resource helping me understand the motivations behind many of the players featured in *Ghosts of the American Revolution*.

Several books on New England's paranormal history were used and cited throughout the text. Other New England–based websites and periodicals, such as Peter Muise's *New England Folklore*, Albert L. Haskell's *Historical Guidebook of Somerville*, Charles M. Skinner's *Myths & Legends of Our Own Land*, History.com, HauntedHouses.com, as well as the websites for the Danvers Historical Society, KYW Newsradio, Harvard's Adams House, and the National Park Service served as sources.

Most of the experts featured in this book, including Christopher Rondina, Gare Allen, Jack Kenna, Joni Mayhan, Michelle Hamilton, Peter Muise, and Tim Weisberg are also authors and I highly recommend their works as supplemental reading.

For the majority of *Ghosts of the American Revolution*, I conducted first-hand interviews, and some of the material is drawn from my own research. My former history-based tours including Boston Haunts and Cambridge Haunts in Harvard Square were also major sources and generated original content. It should be noted that ghost stories are subjective, and I have made a concerted effort to stick to the historical

Historic map on display at the Oliver House in Middleboro, Massachusetts. *Photo by Frank C. Grace*

facts, even if it resulted in debunking an alleged encounter with the paranormal.

Baltrusis, Sam. *Ghosts of Boston: Haunts of the Hub*. Charleston, SC: The History Press, 2012.

———. *Ghosts of Salem: Haunts of the Witch City*. Charleston, SC: The History Press, 2014.

———. *Ghost Writers: The Hallowed Haunts of Unforgettable Literary Icons*. Guilford, CT: Globe Pequot, 2019.

———. *Haunted Boston Harbor*. Charleston, SC: The History Press, 2016.

———. *13 Most Haunted Crime Scenes Beyond Boston*. Boston, MA: Sam Baltrusis, 2016.

———. *Wicked Salem: Exploring Lingering Lore and Legends*. Guilford, CT: Globe Pequot, 2019.

D'Agostino, Thomas. *A Guide to Haunted New England*. Charleston, SC: The History Press, 2009.

D'Entremont, Jeremy. *The Lighthouse Handbook New England*. Kennebunkport, ME: Cider Mill Press, 2016.

Dudley, Dorothy. *Theatrum Majorum: The Cambridge of 1776*. Whitefish, MT: Kessinger Publishing, 2007.

Fiedel, Dorothy Burtz. *Ghosts and Other Mysteries*. Ephrata, PA: Science Press, 1997.

Forest, Christopher. *North Shore Spirits of Massachusetts*. Atglen, PA: Schiffer Publishing, 2003.

French, Allen. *The First Year of the American Revolution*. Boston, MA: Houghton Mifflin, 1934.

Guiley, Rosemary Ellen. *Haunted Salem*. Mechanicsburg, PA: Stackpole Books, 2011.

Hall, Thomas. *Shipwrecks of Massachusetts Bay*. Charleston, SC: The History Press, 2012.

Hauk, Dennis William. *Haunted Places: The National Directory*. New York: Penguin Group, 1996.

Hill, Frances. *Hunting for Witches*. Carlisle, MA: Commonwealth Editions, 2002.

Hugh, Howard. *Houses of the Founding Fathers*. New York: Artisan, 2007.

Kleespies, Gavin W., and Michael Kenney. *Rediscovering the Hooper-Lee-Nichols House*. Cambridge, MA: Cambridge Historical Society, 2010.

Mayhan, Joni. *Dark and Scary Things*. Gardner, MA: Joni Mayhan, 2015.

Muise, Peter. *Legends and Lore of the North Shore*. Charleston, SC: The History Press, 2014.

Nadler, Holly Mascott. *Ghosts of Boston Town: Three Centuries of True Hauntings*. Camden, ME: Down East Books, 2002.

Philbrick, Nathaniel. *Bunker Hill: A City, A Siege, A Revolution*. New York, NY: Penguin Books, 2014.

Powers, Edwin. *Crime and Punishment in Early Massachusetts*. Boston, MA: Beacon Press, 1966.

Rapaport, Diane. *The Naked Quaker: True Crimes and Controversies*. Beverly, MA: Commonwealth Editions, 2007.

Revai, Cheri. *Haunted Massachusetts: Ghosts and Strange Phenomena of the Bay State*. Mechanicsburg, PA: Stackpole Books, 2005.

Rondina, Christopher. *Legends of Sleepy Hollow*. Newport, RI: Ghost Boy Press, 2019.

Rooney, Ashley E. *Cambridge, Massachusetts: Ghosts, Legends & Lore*. Atglen, PA: Schiffer Publishing, 2009.

Rule, Leslie. *When the Ghost Screams: True Stories of Victims Who Haunt*. Kansas City, MO: Andrews McMeel Publishing, 2006.

Stansfield, Charles A. *Haunted Presidents*. Mechanicsburg, PA: Stackpole Books, 2010.

Sweester, M.F. *King's Handbook of Boston Harbor*. Boston, MA: Houghton, Mifflin & Co., 1888.

Zwicker, Roxie J. *Haunted Pubs of New England: Raising Spirits of the Past*. Charleston, SC: The History Press, 2007.

INDEX

ABOUT THE AUTHOR

Author **SAM BALTRUSIS** is a sought-after lecturer who speaks at dozens of paranormal-related events scattered throughout New England. He appears on several television shows including, *The Curse of Lizzie Borden* and *Fright Club* on Discovery+. He is also the producer of the MASS ParaCon and hosts *Paranormal Rewind* and the *Haunted Hotels with Sam Baltrusis* podcasts. Visit SamBaltrusis.com for more information.

Doppelgänger? Author Sam Baltrusis specializes in historical haunts and has been featured on several national television shows sharing his experiences with the paranormal. *Photo by Frank C. Grace*

CPSIA information can be obtained
at www.ICGtesting.com
Printed in the USA
BVHW072314021021
617982BV00002B/4